THE
TRADE AND SHIPPING
OF
NINETEENTH-CENTURY
HULL

by
JOYCE M. BELLAMY,
B.Com., Ph.D.
Department of Economics
University of Hull

CONTENTS

Abbreviations

A. & P.	*Accounts and Papers* (House of Commons)
B. of E. (H.B.) P.L.	Bank of England (Hull Branch) Private Letter
H.A.	*Hull Advertiser*
H.B.C., D.M.B.	Hull Banking Company, Directors' Minute Book
H.C.L.	Kingston upon Hull City Library
H. & E.C.H.	*Hull and Eastern Counties Herald*
H.N.	*Hull News*
H. of C.	House of Commons
H. of L.	House of Lords
H.R.	*Hull Rockingham*
H.U.L.	Hull University: Brynmor Jones Library
M. of E.	Minutes of Evidence
M. of P.	Minutes of Proceedings
M.M.	Maritime Museum, Hull
P.R.O.	Public Record Office, London
S.C.	Select Committee
S.P.	Sessional Papers

Introduction

Britain's increasing industrialisation on the eve of the 19th century stimulated a demand for imported raw materials, many of which originated in Northern Europe. Hull's location on the Humber estuary near the eastern seaboard, and its long tradition of mercantile connections in Baltic ports,[1] naturally brought much of this traffic through the port. In return earthenware, ironware, textiles and other commodities produced by British manufacturers were exported. This emphasis on the trade with Northern Europe continued for much of the 19th century, although from the 1870s Hull's trading connections widened considerably and imports began to flow in increasing quantities from North and South America and Africa. By the late 19th century the import trade was far more important than the export in value, although the reverse had been true earlier in the century. This change in emphasis was encouraged by the development of industries at Hull which were established to process many of the imported raw materials. Throughout the century Hull's trade in commodities was accompanied by a significant interest in the fishing industries; in the early decades Hull was the country's premier port engaged in the Northern Whale Fishery and on the eve of the 20th century was emerging as one of the principal trawl-fishing centres of Britain. But there was no apparent connection between them; the ships used for whaling were considerably larger than the early trawling vessels and whereas the whale shipowners originated mainly from Hull, most of the pioneers of the trawl-fishing industry came from Devon and Kent. Whaling from Hull ceased in 1869 at a time when trawling was becoming an increasingly important sector of the port's economy.

Throughout the 19th century the mercantile community of the town fought to improve the transport facilities connecting Hull with its main industrial hinterland and also those within the port itself. Hull has always been in need of good access to the industrial interior of Britain, and especially to the West Riding and Midlands. Thus the leading merchants and citizens of Hull eagerly supported the various schemes to include the port in the national railway framework and continually pressed for an expansion of dock space at home. In 1800 ships frequenting Hull had the choice of two anchorages—the Old Harbour, which comprised the lower, wharfed, reaches of the River Hull, or the first dock, which covered 9¾ acres and was entered from the River Hull. The dock had been opened in 1778 and was owned by the Hull Dock Company. As the 19th century progressed the increase in the annual tonnage of shipping using the port led to a significant expansion in dock facilities; by 1900 nearly 200 acres of water were available. The movement of goods and passengers to and from the port was improved when the first railway link was achieved in 1840 with the opening of the Hull

---

[1] See R. Davis, *The Trade and Shipping of Hull, 1500-1700* (E. Yorks. Local History Series, no. 17) (1964).

and Selby Railway. The mercantile community had to wait, however, until 1869 for a direct line to Doncaster and until 1885 before the Hull, Barnsley and West Riding Junction Railway established a closer link with the Yorkshire coalfield.

Transport difficulties between Hull and its hinterland should not, however, be exaggerated. The early development of the port, before the railway age, was made possible, in part at least, by the development and exploitation of the complex river system which drained into the Humber and later by the building of canals which both supplemented and complemented the rivers. Hull was the focal point of an extensive river and coasting traffic. Many of the 611 vessels, amounting to 68,533 tons, which were registered at the port in 1800[2] were employed in trans-shipping goods along the coast or along the river and canal networks. Hull, indeed, came fifth in the national list of shipping registered, being surpassed only by Sunderland (75,319 tons), Newcastle (140,055), Liverpool (140,633) and London (568,262). Sunderland and Newcastle had large fleets of coasting craft used for coal shipments. By the end of the century Hull's registered shipping had risen to 882 vessels, totalling 241,635 tons, in 1900 and the port came ninth in national tonnages. In relation to the value of trade handled, however, Hull was Britain's third port.

---

[2] D. Macpherson, *Annals of Commerce, Manufactures, Fisheries and Navigation* (1805), vol. iv, p. 535.

I

1800-15

Trade and shipping at Hull between 1800 and 1815, when the Napoleonic War ended, were affected by the blockading of continental ports, but an expansion of whale fishing and also, during part of the time at least, a growth in shipbuilding output from the local yards sustained the port's economy to a considerable extent. An increased demand for naval ships and vessels for the merchant and whaling fleets provided additional employment for the local population, which rose by about 25 per cent between 1801 and 1811, and—although this cannot be ascertained statistically—many of the immigrants were probably attracted by the local developments.

Hull's emphasis on its overseas, coasting and river traffic, and its whale fishing is reflected in the inclusion of nearly 300 locally resident master mariners in Battle's *Hull Directory* for 1803. Fifty persons were also specifically designated as shipowners although, as elsewhere, shipowning was widespread and often combined with other activities. At least another 300 persons were engaged in mercantile pursuits either as general merchants or specialists in a particular commodity. The wood trade provided work for about 25 merchants, there were about the same number of dealers in wines and spirits, and there were three iron merchants. These included Joseph Sykes & Sons who were, for a time, the sole importers of the high grade Dannemora ore from Sweden, which produced the best quality steel and was used by Sheffield cutlers. Sufficient commercial business was available to maintain at least 40 agents and this also helped to sustain the town's five bankers.[3]

Wood imports figured prominently in the port's trading activities and included various types, such as battens and deals, used mainly for flooring, staves for cask manufacture, and timber for housebuilding and shipbuilding. These imports came mainly from Memel, other Baltic ports, Archangel, and Christiana (now Oslo). It has been estimated that about ten per cent of the battens, boards, deals and deal ends imported at English and Scottish ports in 1800 were landed at Hull.[4] Other imports at Hull included flax, hemp, linseed, tallow, tow and tar, all mainly from Russia, as well as rapeseed from Denmark, bar iron from Sweden and turpentine from America. The growth of British American trade which followed the American War of Independence largely by-passed Hull; in 1800-3 only about three per cent of all foreign vessels arriving at the port were from America.[5] Mediterranean countries supplied barilla (a carbonate of soda derived from the ashes of seaweed and used by bleachers and manufacturers of hard soap and glass), cork and dried fruits. Wines and spirits came mainly from France, Spain and

---

[3] These were: R. W. G. & J. Moxon; Pease, Harrison & Co.; Pease, Knowsley, Wray & Liddell (subsequently Pease & Liddell); Smiths & Thompson; Sykes, Creyke, Broadley & Lockwood (which became Raikes & Co. about 1814).

[4] *A. & P.* 1808 XII.

[5] H.M. Customs, London, 92/29, pp. 117-18.

Portugal. Other imported produce included bristles, mainly from Prussia and Russia, dyestuffs (especially smalts, used in linen, paper and starch manufacture and for staining earthenware, glass and porcelain, which came mainly from Germany and Norway), and clover-seed, groceries, hides, train oil (extracted from fish and from whale blubber), and wheat, primarily from Germany and Prussia but also from Holland.[6] In 1800 over 40 per cent of the bristles and clover-seed, about a third of the bar iron, tow and train oil, 15 per cent of the smalts, and 12 and 10 per cent respectively of the tar and turpentine entering English and Scottish ports arrived at Hull.

In normal years the output of wheat, oats and beans from East Riding farms exceeded local requirements and the surplus was sent principally to the West Riding, Nottinghamshire and London,[7] but poor harvests made augmentation from overseas essential. So far as can be ascertained about ten per cent of the British wheat imports at the turn of the century were landed at Hull. Some of the general merchants at Hull participated in the grain trade but in 1803 the port had only three corn merchants as such, although there were fourteen corn factors; the latter normally acted as intermediaries between farmers and millers. About 20 mills supplied the local residents with flour at this period, including two co-operative milling enterprises: the Hull Anti-Mill Society, established in 1795 to provide cheap flour when the cost of living rose after the onset of the war with France, and the Hull Subscription Mill Society, founded in 1799, also at a time of rising prices.

Local utilisation of Hull's imports cannot be quantified but it seems likely that some would be consumed in Hull mills and work-shops. The street known as Wincolmlee, on the west bank of the River Hull, was described in 1798 as

> One of the most busy streets in or near Hull, in which there are three wind oil mills, one belonging to Messrs. Jarratt and Coates, worked by a steam engine, besides horse mills for the same purpose, a wind saw mill, belonging to Mr. Alderman Os-bourne, the first ever seen in this neighbourhood; a steam en-gine flour mill, constructed on the model of the Albion Mill in London, lately burnt down, but upon a smaller scale. This is truly a curious piece of mechanism, consumes about a chaldron of coals in twelve hours, works four pairs of stones and throws off a vast quantity of flour in a little time. There are likewise in this neighbourhood dry docks and ship yards, where many hands are constantly employed, a large porter brewery, an iron foundry, Greenland houses, tar houses where pitch is made and a sugar house, so that business is carried on in this street to a vast extent; and large quantities of brick and tiles are annually made in the parish for home use and exportation.[8]

[6] L. P. Adams, *Agricultural Depression and Farm Relief in England, 1813-1852* (1932), p. 22; W. F. Galpin, *The Grain Supply of England during the Napol-eonic Period* (1925), p. 134.
[7] H.M. Customs, London, Hull Custom House Outletter Book, 20 Nov. 1800.
[8] J. Tickell, *The History of the Town and County of Kingston upon Hull* (1798), pp. 850-1.

Hull had four oilseed-crushing firms in 1803, at least two of which, Brooke, Pease & Co. and Henry Coates, were importing their own raw materials in 1804. W. Turner, in his *Guide to Hull* (1805), described this industry as 'a very important and lucrative branch of manufacture', but an allied business—paint manufacture—the raw materials of which included colours, linseed oil, white lead (available from a local lead works) and turpentine was, at that time, only in embryo. Largely due to the enterprise of Sissons, Weddle & Co. (later Sissons Bros.), who were making paints by 1804, and Henry Blundell, a brush-maker since 1810 who was making paints by 1813, Hull became an important centre of paint manufacture by mid-century; other firms had also entered this branch of manufacture, which developed into a major local industry by the end of the century.

Other important Hull firms at the start of the 19th century included Todd & Campbell, whose iron foundry sold Dutch tarras (a rock for making mortar or hydraulic cement) and German mill-stones; Thornton, Watson & Co. and Boyes & Carlill, who refined imported sugar, and several which undertook the tanning and currying of leather. John Holmes, a tanner who came to Hull from Doncaster towards the end of the 18th century, was probably attracted to the port by the availability of imported hides. Sail-makers, ropers and tar and turpentine distillers at the port could all utilise imported raw materials, as could the soap-manufacturing firm of Crosse, Escreet & Co. In the early decades of the century, Hull was among the twelve principal soap-making centres of Britain,[9] the raw materials for this product including barilla, rosin and tallow, all of which were handled at the port. The export of British manu-factures through Hull is less well documented, but these included cotton and wool textiles, earthenware, ironware and train oil. The re-export of some imported produce, especially tobacco and spirits, was another facet of Hull's trading activities at the beginning of the 19th century.

*   *   *

The rise in the volume of foreign trade after the end of the American War of Independence not only swelled the tonnage of shipping entering the port but, as at other ports and especially London, Liverpool and Bristol, also gave rise to an increasing demand for additional dock facilities towards the end of the 18th century. Two different locations for a new Hull dock were proposed and in 1793 the Commissioners of H.M. Customs requested three engineers to report on the respective merits of these proposals. The Dock Company recommended a location on the eastern side of the River Hull but a committee of merchants preferred a situation on the western side of the town. The engineers recommended the latter

[9] W. Waterson, *A Cyclopaedia of Commerce* (1846), p. 625. See also *A. & P.* 1827 XVIII; 1833 XXXIII; 1835 XLVIII.

site and in addition one of them suggested a subsequent middle dock to link the Old Dock with the new.

Pressure from local merchants for a second dock was backed by the Customs officials. Early in 1802 (during the Peace of Amiens) the latter complained that 'it is with great difficulty anyone can be brought to the legal quay to deliver her cargo', that the closely-wedged ships were in imminent danger from fire, and that other ships were lying in a dangerous position in the Old Harbour. The agitation led to the passing of the Hull Dock Act of 1802, which authorised the building of a second dock. By 1809, however, when the $7\frac{1}{4}$-acre Humber Dock, opening directly into the Humber, was completed, the volume of traffic using the port had declined substantially below the earlier level. With Hull's trading activities largely directed towards Northern Europe, it was inevitable that the restrictions imposed on overseas trade during the Napoleonic Wars would curtail shipments to and from the port.

The blockading of European ports and the British Government's imposition of a high duty on imports of Baltic wood restricted the timber traffic and the entry of Russia into the war in 1807 on the side of France brought further difficulties to Hull merchants trading with that country. In April 1808 shipping was almost at a standstill and the tonnage of vessels entering Hull from overseas was only 30 per cent of the 1800 total. In 1808, the first year for which data on countries of origin of shipping entering Hull are available (see Table II), nearly half the tonnage came from Sweden, which remained neutral until 1809. Napoleon's attempt through his Continental System to prevent trade with Britain was partially defeated by the use of false papers and assistance from the British navy, so that vessels still entered and departed from Hull on overseas voyages, though to a lesser extent than before. In 1806 Blaydes & Co., Hull merchants and shipowners, had neutral ships sailing direct to Hamburg with cotton goods from MacConnell & Kennedy, one of Manchester's principal cotton exporters, and in 1807 a Boulton and Watt engine succeeded in getting to Rotterdam via Hull, although in the same year Wedgwood pottery destined for Russia could not be embarked.[10] In 1808, however, attempts by British manufacturers to explore other markets were reflected in the shipment to Brazil via Hull of files, tools and other implements from Kirkstall Forge, Leeds.[11]

The tonnage of vessels frequenting Hull rose after 1808 but this was probably due to increased coasting traffic and whale shipping for wartime restrictions were still affecting traffic from overseas in the years 1810 to 1812. Even so, foreign owned vessels were being escorted by the British navy, a policy which aroused much indignation among British shipowners. At Hull meetings were held in 1811 and 1812, and in the latter year the local owners pressed for a full blockade of the Baltic to prevent the use of foreign shipping; some objections to this policy were raised by local timber merchants but the Hull shipowners were backed by local public opinion, which

---

[10] F. Crouzet, *L'Economie Britannique et le Blocus Continentel (1806-1813)* (1958), pp. 169, 228, 254.
[11] Ibid., p. 315.

disliked the 'foreigners'.[12] The fact that whale fishing provided Hull merchants and other local businessmen with opportunities for capital investment, and some of the local population with alternative sources of employment, may have influenced local opinion to support a complete blockade.

Among the vessels registered at Hull in 1801, on which were employed some 3,770 men,[13] were ships being equipped for whaling. Government bounties encouraged this trade. In the mid 18th century 40s. per ton of shipping was paid but this rate was reduced to 20s. in 1795 and was applicable only to ships of over 200 tons. Payments continued at this level until 1824, when the bounties ceased. Merchant ships of from 200 to over 350 tons were refitted for the Hull whaling trade, but new sailing vessels were also acquired from local shipyards, other British builders and abroad. At the turn of the century about 40 per cent of British ships fishing in the Greenland and Davis Straits areas were equipped at Hull and between 1799 and 1802 the number of ships sailing from the port rose from 28 to 36. The whalers usually left Hull in March or April, returning in September or October, although they were often delayed and sometimes had to winter in the Arctic; losses were frequent. Crews of at least 40 men were required and about a third were recruited from the Orkney and Shetland Islands. The trade also provided employment for many hundreds of Hull men[14] and work on building and equipping the ships offered further opportunities for the local male population.

Accurate estimates of capital invested are impossible, but in 1803 a new Whitby whaler of 219 tons cost £7,791, including advance money for the seamen, insurance premiums, outfit and stores, and in 1812 a 350-ton Hull-built ship cost an estimated £14,000 for building and furnishing.[15] Assuming an average of £10,000 per ship, perhaps some £300,000 had been invested in the Hull whaling fleet at the turn of the century. Further investment was undertaken to provide facilities for processing the whale products and 'Greenland' yards for this purpose were located alongside the River Hull, the whaler's cargoes being conveyed there by lighters. The whale blubber was then boiled down to provide oil for lamps, soap manufacture, the preparation of leather and coarse woollen cloths, varnish and paint manufacture and machinery lubrication. Various ornaments and articles of dress were made from some of the bone, the remainder being crushed for manure or, in the case of the jawbones, used as gateposts by farmers or to

[12] A. N. Ryan, 'Trade with the Enemy in the Scandinavian and Baltic Ports during the Napoleonic War: for and against', *Trans. Royal Historical Society*, 5th series, vol. 12 (1962), pp. 129-132; *A Full Report of the Proceedings at Two Meetings of the Merchants, Shipowners, etc. at Kingston-upon-Hull, April 4 1811 and February 11 1812, respecting the Granting of Licenses to Foreign Ships; Together with a Copy of the Memorial laid before the Board of Trade; and the Petition presented to the House of Commons* (1812).

[13] W. Gawtress, *Report of an Inquiry into the Corporation of Hull* (1834), p. 384.

[14] It has been estimated from data published in J. R. McCulloch, *Dictionary of Commerce* (1837), p. 1241, that the Hull whale ships in 1802 would employ some 1,400 men, although the number of local residents cannot be ascertained.

[15] Capt. Scoresby, *The Northern Whale Fishery* (1835), p. 155; J. Leslie, *Narrative of Discovery and Adventure in the Polar Seas and Regions* (1835), p. 442.

form ornamental archways. From part of the offal glue was extracted, and a fibrous substance, similar to horsehair, was used for stuffing chairs.[16]

The number of ships equipped for the whale fisheries rose to 48 in 1814-15. Between 1800 and 1815 nearly 30 Hull whalers were lost at sea or captured by the enemy but were replaced by new ships from local yards or elsewhere. A scarcity of tallow supplies anticipated on Russia's entry into the war provided further justification for pursuing the whale, since whale oil could be used for lamps and was therefore a substitute for tallow candles. In 1812 a quarter of the shipping tonnages entering Hull from overseas came from the whale fisheries and, assuming that all were registered at Hull, they represented about a fifth of the ships belonging to the port in 1812-15. Owners of ships used for whaling included not only merchants and insurance brokers but some of the shipbuilders, such as Edward Gibson and Thomas Walton. Other local businessmen who participated in the trade were G. & J. Eggington, oil merchants and seed-crushers, Spyvee & Cooper, ropers, Thomas Carlill, cabinet maker, William Shackles, draper, and William Lee, tar and turpentine distiller. The gross value of the products of the whale fishery has been estimated at nearly £240,000 in 1814 (see Table III) and the whale shipowners had become prominent members of the mercantile community. At least in the years 1813 to 1825, which marked the greatest local participation in the trade, and probably for a longer period, the Whale Shipowners' Association was actively engaged in protecting its members' interests. In 1815 the Association petitioned the Lords of the Treasury against rapeseed imports,[17] rape oil, like tallow, being competitive with whale oil for lighting and other uses. The petition was also sent to all ports with ships sailing to the fisheries, requesting their co-operation. How far this early 'pressure group' influenced the Government's decision to increase the rapeseed duty in 1816 is not known because there was severe agricultural distress at the time and some protection for the rapeseed-growing areas of Britain was justified; some Yorkshire oil-millers, however, pressed for rapeseed imports to be duty free.[18]

Shipbuilding was already well-established at Hull by the beginning of the 19th century. Although contemporary shipbuilding data are somewhat misleading, they show that Hull was at the centre of one of the major British shipbuilding areas. In 1801, for example, 87 ships, totalling 10,876 tons, were built in the Hull 'port area'[19] and registered at Hull, which was second only to the premier port,

[16] G. Head, *A Home Tour through the Manufacturing Districts of England, in the Summer of 1835* (1836), p. 247.
[17] Minute Book of the Whaling Shipowners' Association, 1813-25: M.M.
[18] H. of C. Journal, vol. 71. The petition of the oil-millers presented on 2 April 1816 was referred to the Committee on Agricultural Distress and on 12 June 1816 a duty of £10 per last was agreed, the earlier duties having been repealed.
[19] For Customs purposes, which included the registration of ships, the Hull port area comprised such out-lying river ports as Gainsborough, Goole, Selby, Thorne and other places in Yorkshire and Lincolnshire adjacent to the Humber and statistics of ships built and registered at Hull include some built in yards at the out-ports.

London.[20] Ships were built in six yards along the River Hull: at North End, South End, Old Dock Bridge, Lime Street (two) and Church Street. A seventh, at Great Union Street, was opened in 1804. The Gleadow and Walton families and William Gibson were the principal shipbuilders. Other firms described as boat-builders were also located along the banks of the Rivers Hull and Humber.

The Hull shipyards benefited in the early 19th century from orders for naval vessels and for whalers. From plans drawn up for the Navy Board by John Staniforth, M.P. for Hull in 1802-18, several ships were built in Hull yards for the Royal Navy[21] and nearly 30 of the Hull-built merchant ships participated in the whaling trade. Ships built and registered in the Hull 'port area' in 1806 and 1813 exceeded the tonnage at any of the other English shipbuilding centres. At Hull itself, in 1810, at least fourteen ships, totalling 3,500 tons, were built in local yards, of which several were destined for the whaling trade. The shipping registered at Hull in 1813 was nearly 89,000 tons and gave employment to 5,553 seamen, but registered tonnages in the early decades of the century were probably over-estimated. A new Registry Act (4 Geo. IV, c. 41) obliged all vessel owners to register them anew. Prior to 1827 all ships registered were presumed to exist until contrary evidence was shown, and data relating to the years before 1827 may therefore have been in excess of the actual tonnage belonging to the port.

In the first decade or so of the 19th century Hull, like other ports, was on the eve of the steamship era. As early as 1788 William Symington, a country millwright, had built a paddle ship driven by a steam engine.[22] In the same year two men from Elland, in the West Riding, Robert Fourness and James Ashworth, obtained the first patent for a steam engine to work and tow sloops and barges.[23] It has not been possible to prove the assertion that Hull was the location for the construction of the first steam packet in England,[24] but steam propulsion of vessels was definitely recorded in 1814, when a steamboat was reported to be 'exhibiting her capabilities' on the River Humber, and in 1815 the *Caledonia* steam packet travelled from York to Hull via the Ouse and Humber.[25] In the latter year the Humber steam packet conveyed passengers 55 miles from Hull to Selby and took five hours for the journey, linking with coaches from Leeds and Wakefield.

Of the financial effects of the Napoleonic Wars on Hull's economy little is known, but there is evidence of failures among merchants trading with Russia. In addition, the bankers Pease & Co.

---

[20] H. of L. (in 91 of 1814-15) LXXV.
[21] *H.A.* 24 Nov. and 8 Dec. 1804; *S.C.* on the Navigation Laws, *M. of E.* Appendix E.e. No. 5, 1847-8 XX Pt. II.
[22] See G. R. Porter, *The Progress of the Nation* (1851), p. 315, for early developments in the application of steam power.
[23] P.R.O. C66/3842/2, Patent no. 1640, 4 Mar. 1788.
[24] J. J. Sheahan, *History of the Town and Port of Kingston-upon-Hull* (1st edn. 1864), p. 584.
[25] *H.R.* 15 Oct. 1814, 13 May 1815.

experienced losses[26] and in 1815 the bank of Moxon & Co. closed down. At the end of the war, however, the whale fishery was well-established and the increased demand for naval ships and vessels for the merchant and whaling fleets had provided additional employment for the local population. By 1815 inward tonnages from overseas had regained their 1800 level and almost 90 per cent of the tonnages (excluding ships from the whale fisheries) came from Northern Europe. Of the North European total, nearly 40 per cent was from Russia. Outside Europe Hull's trade connections were mainly with the British North American colonies, whence came wood to supplement the much reduced Baltic imports, purposely restricted by high British tariffs imposed in the war years.

Hull was being increasingly used for shipments of cotton twist, cotton manufactures and woollen goods to continental Europe, especially Germany, the Netherlands and Russia. In 1815 nearly two-thirds of British cotton twist passed through Hull but cotton piece goods sent via Hull were only five per cent of national exports in that year. It was the cotton traffic which gave rise, in the 1830s, to the establishment of cotton manufacture in Hull, a development which belongs to the next section.

---

[26] J. A. S. L. Leighton-Boyce, *Smiths the Bankers, 1658-1958* (1958), p. 228; F. Crouzet, *L'Economie Britannique*, p. 833.

II

1816-40

Between 1815 and 1840, when the opening of the Hull and Selby Railway linked the port with the national railway network, Hull's economy was still primarily mercantile. The volume of shipping using the port largely reflected national trends, with peaks in 1818, 1825 and 1839, but by 1840 whaling had declined. The general economic depression of the late 1820s was particularly acute in Hull; fewer whalers sailed from the port and the output from the local shipyards was greatly reduced. For each year from 1826 to 1832 withdrawals exceeded deposits at the Hull Savings Bank, which was opened in 1818 to provide facilities for the poorer members of the community. From the mid-1830s, on the other hand, Hull shared in the general improvement in the British economy. The volume of shipping frequenting the port increased, previous tonnages being exceeded, shipbuilding expanded once more, new seed-crushing firms were established, and local merchants, impressed by the volume of cotton textiles being shipped from Hull, established a cotton mill company in the town. By 1841 Hull had a population of 67,308 and, whereas Manchester and most of the larger English towns had 'grown more rapidly between 1821 and 1831 than they were ever to grow again',[27] at Hull it was the thirties which showed the most rapid growth in the first half of the century.

*   *   *

British overseas trade grew rapidly with the end of hostilities in 1815 and by 1818 shipping tonnages at Hull exceeded the level specified in the Dock Act of 1802 for the building of a third dock. Prominent merchants and shipowners formed a local committee in December 1818 to join representatives of Hull Corporation and the Trinity House in discussions with the Hull Dock Company. The latter agreed initially to provide half the money and the committee recommended that the remainder should be obtained by a government loan secured by additional dues on shipping. An increase of 25 per cent on the rates paid by foreign vessels was suggested and also a tonnage duty on the export of goods and a duty of 2d. per ton on all river sloops, loading or delivering at the port. The annual volume of this river shipping was estimated in 1819 at 230,000 tons.[28] The revenue from these sources was expected to provide sufficient return to pay the interest on the loan and extinguish the debt within fifteen years of completion of the dock. The Company would not accept this proposal but offered to provide the total cost on condition, *inter alia*, that the proposed duty on river vessels be granted permanently to the Dock Company. This attempt by the Company to secure a permanent charge on river traffic, previously untaxed, was refuted and when trade declined shortly afterwards the proposal was shelved.

---

[27] J. H. Clapham, *An Economic History of Modern Britain*, vol. 1 (2nd edn. 1939) (reprinted 1959), p. 536.
[28] Committee for obtaining additional Dock Room, *Report*, 22 Feb. 1819.

In 1824, however, after two years of expanding trade, a local committee was again formed to report on plans for a third dock. The Company agreed to build it and specified the levying of a scale of duties on the shipping using the port. Opposition to the proposals was then encountered from some of the property-owners on the Old Harbour who objected to increased dock dues. Among the prime movers in this agitation was S. T. Hassell, a local merchant. By enlisting support from other parts of Britain, the opposition achieved the withdrawal of the parliamentary Bill in 1825—an action deplored by the *Hull Rockingham*, in the editorial columns of which on 27 August 1825 there appeared a plea for the leading interests in the town to 'lay aside all animosity and private feeling, meet together in the spirit of patriotism and try what can be done'. This point of view was to be re-echoed throughout the century in relation to the provision of dock and transport facilities. The opposition's influence was, at that time, short-lived, for in 1826 the Dock Company decided to build the dock with the aid of a loan from the Exchequer Loan Commissioners. In 1829 Junction Dock, connecting Humber and Old Docks, was opened, increasing to nearly 23 acres the dock area of the port.

The 1825 trade boom which brought 328,000 tons of shipping into Hull from overseas—two and a half times the 1815 total and a tenth of the tonnage entering all British ports—was primarily the consequence of government policies and the outbreak of a speculation mania. It gave to Hull a relative share of national overseas trade not again achieved in the 19th century (see Table I). The Government had amended the Navigation Laws and entered into reciprocal agreements with Denmark, Norway, Prussia, Sweden, and the ports of Bremen and Hamburg which reduced the duty payable by foreign vessels relative to those of British ownership. This policy encouraged the use of foreign ships. In addition, import duties payable on iron and rapeseed were substantially reduced. Imports of these and other products from Northern Europe increased and, apart from London, Hull was the principal east coast port handling this traffic. The number of foreign ships entering Hull rose from 205 in 1823 to 1,000 in 1825, whereas British vessels increased at a substantially lower rate, from 779 to 1,175. The number of foreign vessels at Hull, amounting to some 46 per cent of the vessels using the port in 1825, was proportionately greater than for the country as a whole, where only 34 per cent were of foreign origin. Hull shipowners had formed their own association in 1823 and, following the influx of foreign vessels, members of the Hull Shipowners' Association petitioned Parliament in 1827 on the detrimental effect which the amendment of the Navigation Laws was having on their interests.[29]

The speculative boom, which affected the whole country in the mid-1820s, collapsed towards the close of 1825; there were some commercial failures and many country bankers had to stop payments. At Hull, however, no bank failures were reported and the

---

[29] *H.A.* 23 Mar. 1827.

columns of the *Hull Advertiser* for 16 December 1825 contained the comment that 'the late distress in London and elsewhere has had very little effect in producing any runs upon the banking houses of this town, all of whom . . . were fully prepared to meet even more than any demand that could be made upon them'. Nevertheless, while none of the Hull banks closed its doors, local merchants had been dependent upon banking assistance during this period of over-trading. Some of the major commodities handled at the port—including hides, seeds, tallow, wines and spirits, and wood—had to be paid for promptly by bills at two months credit, although others—including flax, hemp, iron, lead, pitch, tar and turpentine—were subject to six months credit.

That the local merchants had a great respect for their bankers was apparent in 1827 when, following the 1826 Bank Act which empowered the Bank of England to open branches, the Bank decided to establish a Hull branch. This proposal aroused considerable consternation among the banking and mercantile community of the port and Thomas Thompson (of Smiths & Thompson's bank) informed the Bank of England in May 1827 that the 'town and neighbourhood would not be benefited by the establishment of a Branch Bank there'. Smiths & Thompson's was probably the principal Hull bank in the early decades of the 19th century and its customers included J. Sykes & Sons, the iron merchants, the Hull Dock Company and the Collector of Customs. Opposition to the proposal was also expressed by some of the local merchants in a letter to Samuel Thornton, of the sugar-refining firm of Thornton, Watson & Co., who was then a Bank of England director. They indicated their support for the private banks, commenting that they

> are not only possessed of ample and sufficient means to support and facilitate our Commerce, but the regularity and prudence with which we know they are conducted and their engagements being kept within easy reach of their means, creates on our part a confidence which we not easily could give to any other establishment and we owe it to them, in full justice for the assistance and services they rendered the Town at the late period of peculiar distress and pressure, and from our know-ledge of their means and their inclinations to support them against any competition.

This letter, of 6 September 1827, was signed by the Mayor, J. Sykes & Sons, and many other gentlemen and firms.[30]

Despite the local opposition the Bank of England proceeded with its plans and a branch was opened in 1829. Correspondence between the Hull agent and the Bank in London emphasised the dependence of the local mercantile community on Hull bankers. Shortly after his tenure of office commenced, the agent informed the Bank that

> where confidence existed and the capital and respectability of the parties were beyond dispute, *any* bills, to almost any amount were received and a heavy cash advance was made

---

[30] B. of E. Branch Bank Committee minutes, 27 Sept. 1827.

from time to time for temporary purposes, in addition to the amount of such bills. The banker was usually under a cash advance to his mercantile customer. He was repaid for this by ¼ per cent commission on every transaction and 5 per cent on all advances. Irregularity or suspicion of accommodation formed no objection to the receipt of bills, provided there was one good name. With inferior houses business was done on the same principles, but, of course, with more caution. In many instances tottering houses have been supported by accommodation paper and renewal of bills, long after their situation was desperate, till the banker had an opportunity of saving himself ... The capital of Hull is not large in proportion to the business done here, and, in consequence of the over-trading to which the above system mainly contributed, the pressure and distress in 1825-6 was *very* great. The bankers had recourse, no doubt necessarily, to very harsh and severe measures to enforce payment of their advances. Great sacrifices were made, but one way or other all the parties got through the difficulty except two or three of no credit or repute whose affairs were previously bad.[31]

This considerable dependence upon bank finance became increasingly apparent during subsequent decades, especially among some of the more speculative members of the mercantile community.

*   *   *

Hull's import trade in the 1820s and 1830s resembled the pattern of earlier decades, but although the tonnage of shipping entering the docks from Russian ports was some 71,000 tons in 1840 —compared with 41,000 in 1815—it represented only a fifth of total inward tonnages, compared with nearly 40 per cent in 1815 (see Table II). By 1840 shipping entering from Denmark, Germany, the Netherlands and Prussia was proportionately higher than in 1815 but the overall share from Northern Europe in 1840 was nine per cent less than in the earlier year, due largely to government fiscal policy. The threat of a timber famine when Napoleon extended his Continental system to Northern Europe in 1809-10 provoked the British Government to raise the duties on European timber from 25s. a load to 54s. 8d.; they were further raised to 65s. in 1813 on the pretext of a need to increase the revenue. Colonial timber was admitted tax free from 1806 to 1821, when a duty of 10s. per load was imposed, the duty on European timber being reduced to 55s. This policy, designed to encourage wood imports from British colonial territories, was continued, though in modified form, to mid-century and radically changed the pattern of this trade; about three-quarters of total U.K. wood imports came from these colonies in the early 1830s. At Hull the inwards traffic from British North America (Canada, New Brunswick, Nova Scotia and Prince Edward Island) increased from four per cent of total inwards tonnage from overseas in 1815 to sixteen per cent in 1835 and fourteen per cent in

---

[31] B. of E. (H.B.) P.L. 29, 18 Apr. 1829.

1840. Some of the wood was actually shipped from Baltic to North American ports and then returned to Hull, the timber duties being so high on Baltic timber that the differences in the prices of the two sources of supply were 'about sufficient to indemnify the enormous expense of this round-about voyage'.[32]

Russia and Prussia were still the principal sources of wheat imports. The quantities imported fluctuated widely from year to year depending on the size of the home harvests. Failures in the home crops in 1829-31 encouraged imports in those years but the quantity imported in the mid-thirties was negligible. Imports rose again in 1838 and in the following year British wheat and flour imports were nearly five times the 1821-37 average. At Hull, a convenient port for this trade, imports rose to 429,000 quarters in 1839, a level not exceeded until 1862. The grain trade was notoriously speculative, a situation encouraged by the government policy of establishing sliding scales of duties designed to protect British farmers. In 1828, for example, when Parliament amended earlier scales, imported wheat was liable to a duty of 32s. 8d. per quarter when British wheat was at 54s. As British wheat prices rose, the rates of duty payable declined, but this policy encouraged speculation among importers who were able to benefit when prices rose, since they had to pay less duty on their stocks of wheat. The inherent financial dangers in the grain trade were emphasised in September 1839 when the Bank of England warned the Hull agent about the large bills of exchange being drawn between corn factors and millers which the Bank inferred were

> probably for the purpose of enabling them to force up the price of British wheat, that the foreign corn imported by them may be released at the low duty. If the continuance of the present unfavourable weather should further the object they may realize large profits, but you must bear in mind that speculations in the Corn Trade are proverbially hazardous and under any circumstances you will not be justified in passing any name as our security unless you have reason to believe that his property is fully equal to the total amount drawn, accepted or endorsed by him for which you hold him liable.[33]

Some of the principal corn importers, such as Taylor, Clifford & Bright, William West, Henry Roberts & Co., Sugar & Gray, and S. F. & G. Burstall, did make large profits but by 1842 the two last-named firms had failed. Hall's, Todd & Hassell, general merchants who also dealt in corn, experienced heavy losses in 1838. The Bank of England had granted the firm discounting facilities for bills of exchange up to £5,000 in value but this was reduced to £2,000 in 1839.

Increased quantities of raw wool were among the principal imports of the 1820s and 1830s. Expansion in the British woollen textile industry created a demand for raw wool in excess of the home clip. As Germany was initially the main source and as Hull was close

---

[32] *A. & P.* 1834 XLIX; McCulloch, *Dictionary of Commerce*, p. 1153.
[33] B. of E. (H.B.) P.L. 117, 19 Sept. 1839.

to the wool textile districts of West Yorkshire, the port's location favoured this trade. From 1821, when 2.1 mill. lbs. entered the port, to 1825, when the quantity rose to 11.7 mill. lbs., Hull's share of British wool imports doubled (from 13 to 27 per cent); during the following decade, when imports increased still further, the port handled a third of British imports in some years.

In the late 1830s linseed imports also increased and were over three times those of earlier years in the decade; rapeseed imports had more than doubled, stimulated by the tariff reduction of 1825 and an increased demand for cattle food. Imports at Hull were also influenced by an expansion of the local seed-crushing industry. Henry Blundell, one of the principal paint manufacturers, became actively interested in the industry, which supplied one of his basic raw materials—linseed oil. After taking over a patent for a machine for grinding or crushing oilseeds, obtained in 1827 by a William Benecke on behalf of a William Pescatore, of Luxemburg, Blundell obtained a patent in 1830 for his own improvements to the machine. He also improved on the early hydraulic presses by increasing the size of the rams which were driven on to the boxes containing the seed. He made a press containing four boxes known as 'Blundell's Patent Boxes', although no patent specification for these has been found. By 1831 Hull had eight firms of seed-crushers and by 1838 the number had risen to thirteen. In the late 1820s Todd & Campbell's foundry (known locally as the Old Foundry) supplied oil presses to Pease, Trigg & Co., seed-crushers, and similar equipment was being sold in 1839 by W. Oldham & Son, Hull engineers, who advertised 'a double hydraulic press, together with pumps and driving gear made by Fenton, Murray & Jackson [of Leeds] and fitted with Blundell's Patent Boxes for eight cakes'.

Allied to seed-crushing was bone-grinding, the dust being used as a fertiliser, especially in turnip cultivation. Bones were also used for knife handles and button moulds but the principal consumers of the bones imported through Hull, one of the main ports for this traffic in the post-1815 period, were the farmers of the Yorkshire and Lincolnshire Wolds. In 1815 8,000 tons of bones were imported at Hull, some of which may have come via the coastal trade rather than from continental ports. Hull itself had several bone-mills but a substantial business was conducted in the trans-shipment of bones which, in the 1820s and subsequent decades, came from Europe. A graphic account of this traffic was published in *The Observer* of 18 November 1822 under the heading of 'War and Commerce', where it was

> estimated that more than a million bushels of human and inhuman bones were imported last year from the continent of Europe into the port of Hull. The neighbourhood of Leipsig, Austerlitz, Waterloo and of all the places where . . . the principal battles were fought, have been swept alike of the bones of the hero and of the horse which he rode. Thus collected from every quarter, they have been shipped to the port of Hull, and thence forwarded to the Yorkshire bone grinders, who have erected steam engines and powerful machinery, for the purpose

of reducing them to a granulary state. In this condition they are
... sold to the farmers to manure their lands.[34]
The trade was still extensive in the 1830s, an annual average of
25,000 tons being landed at Hull in 1835-40, about twice the
weight of the iron bars imported in 1835.

The tonnage of shipping leaving Hull in ballast declined from
75 per cent in 1825 to 42 per cent in 1832, an indication of the port's
increased share in Britain's export trade. In 1833, the first year for
which complete value data are available, exports from Hull were
worth £5.2 mill., being thirteen per cent of the U.K. total. Four
years later their value had risen to £8.8 mill. and represented a
fifth of the declared value of British exports. Inevitably the pattern
of Hull's export trade reflected that of British exports to Northern
Europe (see Diagram I). With cotton goods accounting for about
45 per cent of the declared value of British exports in the 1830s,
Hull was a natural gateway for much of this traffic, especially cotton
twist and yarn. These exports were destined mainly for European
markets and in 1835 Hull accounted for 70 per cent of U.K. yarn
exports. Cotton piece goods, on the other hand, were sold mainly to
China, North and South America, the East and West Indies and the
Mediterranean lands—countries with which Hull had few trade
links—and only ten per cent of these exports passed through the port.

It was, however, the growth of this cotton traffic which
induced some of Hull's merchants to invest locally in cotton
manufacture. Three general merchants, Messrs. Hall, Hassell and
Pease, a timber merchant, Mr. Youle, a corn merchant, Mr. Taylor,
(of Taylor, Clifford & Bright), and a commission agent, Mr.
Staniland, were the first directors of the Hull Flax and Cotton Mill
Company. This was formed in 1836 with an authorised capital of
£100,000 in shares of £100, and land adjoining the River Hull was
acquired. The local merchant, S. T. Hassell, was appointed
chairman of the company with Joseph Rylands, a flax and cotton
manufacturer from Wigan, as chief manager. Workers were brought
from Manchester 'in boat-loads'[35] when spinning operations
commenced in 1838, as the Hull and Selby Railway had not yet been
opened. By 1840 raw cotton for the mill was imported at Hull and
between 800 and 900 workers were employed. The arrival of these
workers and their families contributed significantly towards Hull's
population growth in the 1830s.

Other textile exports from Hull included linen and silk goods,
woollen cloth and yarn, lace and net. Other commodities shipped
from the port included iron and steel goods, hardware, machinery,
tinplate and small quantities of coal. Local industries, in addition to
the cotton mills, also contributed to the export traffic. Henry
Blundell, for example, dispatched to Rio de Janiero in 1832 tins of
paint, painters' colours, red and white lead, lamp black, soda,

---

[34] I am indebted to Dr. W. M. Mathew, of Leicester Univ., for information on
this traffic and to Dr. W. H. Chaloner, of Manchester Univ., for the quotation
from *The Observer*.
[35] A passenger steam-packet service operated between Hull and Selby; see below
p. 34.

Epsom salts, linseed oil, painters' brushes and varnishes. His products were also destined for New York and Cadiz. G. & T. Earle, who commenced as Russia merchants in 1809, were making cement by 1821 and sending Paris white to New York in the early 1830s. Other miscellaneous exports included 'a common lathe', umbrellas, gigs and a phaeton. These could have been local products: King & Co., ironmongers, specialised in lathe manufacture and Hull had umbrella- and carriage-makers at that time.

★ ★ ★

In the early 1820s plans were being made for the building of the Stockton and Darlington Railway and, with the improvement in trade at that time, an enthusiasm for investment in such schemes developed in many parts of the country. By early 1825, committees had been formed in Hull and Leeds to discuss the establishment of a railway connection between the two towns. The Hull committee included G. Liddell, banker, A. Terry, a prominent merchant, and a shipowner, S. Gee. The subsequent financial crisis temporarily caused this scheme to be shelved, but in 1828 support was given to a proposed railway between Leeds and Selby at the same time as Hull merchants and bankers were financing a scheme for a steam packet and tug service between Hull and Selby. The merchants of Hull were always sensitive to developments in facilities in the rest of Humberside and when the first docks at Goole, which had been built for the Aire and Calder Navigation Company, were opened for river and coastal vessels in 1826 the effect on the volume of coasting trade passing through Hull was immediate. Between 1827 and 1828 the number of coasting vessels entering the Hull docks declined from 3,596 to 1,641. In 1828, when the Goole port facilities were available for foreign trade, the Hull Dock Company, Hull Corporation and the Trinity House subscribed £1,000 each for a Hull to Selby packet and tug scheme. Other Hull shareholders included bankers, merchants, shipowners and the seed-crushers, Pease, Trigg & Co. Steam tugs were operated between Hull and Selby in the 1830s by the Hull and Selby Steam Tug Co. and passengers were carried on the steam packets of the Hull and Selby Steam Co. Sir George Head's contemporary account of this passenger service vividly described the inconvenience experienced by travellers, when in an attempt to prevent the vessel sticking in the mud

> the captain received the able support from all his passengers who, about forty in number condescendingly acted in concert under his directions and shuffled across from one side to another so as to keep her going . . . Whenever in a coarse gruff voice, he gave the emphatic word of command 'Rowl her', the crowd, like sheep at the bark of a dog, trotted across the deck treading on one another's heels and suffering much personal inconvenience. At the same time they hauled upon a rope, previously sent on shore and made fast to a purchase, till the vessel was disengaged from her soft bed and again afloat in a channel nearer the shore.[36]

---

[36] G. Head, *A Home Tour*, pp. 212-13.

On this particular occasion the boat became completely stuck for three hours and the journey which had begun from Selby at 8 a.m. ended at Hull at 6 p.m. Even on arrival at Hull, when the water was low, landing was very inconvenient and passengers had either to climb a perpendicular ladder or to 'walk a rickety plank from ship to shore'.

The existence of this service, although subject to delay and uncertainty, probably retarded by several years the establishment of direct railway communications between Hull and the rest of the country. Liverpool was linked with Manchester by 1830 and the Leeds to Selby line had opened in 1834, in the same year that the Hull and Selby Railway Company was formed to promote the building of the line to Hull. An East Riding landowner, Henry Broadley, was chairman of the provisional committee and James Gadsden, sugar refiner and director of the Yorkshire District Bank, was deputy chairman. By October 1834 £150,000 of the £350,000 authorised capital was subscribed. At least 70 per cent of its first shareholders—of whom there were 100 individuals and Hull Corporation—were local merchants, bankers, shipowners and shipbuilders, but they also included a tanner and some drapers. Among the first directors were Henry Broadley, J. C. Parker, chairman of the Hull Dock Company, James Henwood and George Liddell (bankers who, it is said, 'first took up the promotion of the extension of the line from Selby to Hull'),[37] Charles Whitaker, an iron merchant, W. S. Cooper, roper, John Gresham, tailor and draper, Avison Terry, merchant, and Richard Tottie, agent to the Hamburg Steam Packet Co. Of the fifteen elected, seven were shareholders of the Hull Dock Company in that year. On 1 July 1840 the line was officially opened and a regular passenger and parcels service inaugurated the following day. Hull was thereby connected with the West Riding and Lancashire via Leeds and with the Midlands via Leeds, Sheffield and Derby, areas which supplied most of the goods exported from Hull. It was also linked with London via Leeds.

*　　*　　*

Between 1818 and 1832 shipping registered at Hull declined vis-à-vis the U.K.—from 3.5 per cent of the national total to 2.7 per cent. The absolute decline from 87,600 tons may have been influenced by the possible over-estimation of the years prior to 1827 but this downward trend reflected a general decline in whale fishing, which was particularly severe at Hull, and also the trade depression of the late 1820s and early 1830s which affected the local shipowners and Hull shipbuilding yards. While some of the ships previously used for whaling were transferred to general trading, nearly 40 vessels were lost between 1818 and 1835.

Whaling from Hull reached its peak in 1818 when 64 ships returned to the port with catches valued at over £272,000. At least 25 firms had equipped ships for this trade and the principal whale shipowners included C. Bolton, merchant and underwriter, S.

---

[37] G. G. MacTurk, *A History of Hull Railways* (1879), p. 36.

Cooper, roper, G. and J. Eggington, oil merchants and seed-crushers, and J. Marshall, shipowner. With eleven other owners they subscribed towards the establishment of gas manufacture in Hull, obtaining an Act in 1821 for this purpose which permitted the use of whale oil. Before 1830, however, the Kingston upon Hull Gas Co.'s works where the whale oil was used had become a nuisance to the neighbourhood. The gas produced was uneconomic when compared with that of a rival company, the British Gas Light Co., founded in 1826, whose raw material was coal. By 1830 the Kingston Company had stopped using whale oil.

Further expansion in seed-crushing, the products of which were also competitive with whale oil, the loss of nine ships in 1821, and the withdrawal of the government bounty in 1824 were factors deterring the equipping of vessels for the trade. Even so, Hull merchants continued to send large fleets to the fishing grounds. In 1830 33 vessels sailed from Hull and the capital invested in the trade was estimated at not less than £400,000, with 1,500 men employed.[38] In that year, one of the worst in British whaling history, nineteen ships were lost, six of them from Hull. Whales had become scarce and further distances had to be travelled in search of them. London, Britain's premier port in the fishery during the 18th century, had almost abandoned it by 1832 and Liverpool had completely withdrawn by the early 1830s. Hull was slower to reduce its whaling commitments. In 1831, 32 ships returned from the fishing grounds but during the later 1830s numbers declined rapidly. In 1840 only four ships sailed and Hull's share of total U.K. tonnages was only thirteen per cent, compared with 41 per cent in 1818-19. There had been a general decline in whaling tonnage, except at the Scottish ports of Peterhead, Dundee and Leith, where an increased participation in the trade occurred. Their location, some hundreds of miles nearer to the fishing grounds than the other major ports, enabled two trips a year to be made.

In the early 1830s shipping tonnages frequenting the port had increased and in 1835 a committee of owners of property along the Old Harbour considered making it into a dock for sailing vessels and building another dock at its entrance for steam packets. The continued growth of trade in 1836-7 increased the pressure for improved facilities. In 1836 the Hull Dock Company had offered to sell the docks to the town, a proposal accepted by Hull Corporation but rejected by a public meeting of townspeople who were not prepared to shoulder the responsibility for the docks as they were 'afraid of a borough rate'.[39] A prospectus issued in 1838 for a new dock company threatened the monopoly of the existing company, which then proposed the building of another dock. But when a parliamentary committee considering the Hull Docks Bill of 1840 suggested amendments to which the Company objected, the Bill was

[38] *H.A.* 15 Oct. 1830; see also Leslie, *Narrative of Discovery*, pp. 442-4.
[39] T. Wood, *Tidal Harbours Commission, The Humber . . . importance and improvement of the port of Hull: a report of the proceedings at the Town Hall, Hull on 23 October 1845* (n.d.), p. 35.

withdrawn, thereby retarding for some years the expansion of the dock acreage. In the meantime Hull's relative share of national inward tonnages from overseas had declined; from 9.4 per cent for the years 1825-9, which included the exceptional year 1825 when it was 10.6 per cent, to 6.8 per cent for the years from 1840 to 1849 (see Table I).

Some progress was, however, made in the growth of steam shipping at the port. F. H. Pearson, in his *Early History of Hull Steam Shipping* (1896), traces in some detail the pattern of this development so only the main outlines will be given here. The first regular steam shipping service was established in 1821 by the Hull Steam Packet Co., the proprietors of which lived in and around Thorne where their first ship, the S.P. *Kingston*, was built. This vessel was used in the Hull to London trade. Weddle and Brownlow, Hull shipping agents, also held shares in the ships owned by the company and acted as the latter's agents. R. Keddy introduced the S.P. *Lowther* to the coasting trade between Hull, Selby, Goole and Yarmouth in 1824; this vessel, launched in the previous year from a Hull yard, was reported to be the first steam packet to be built at Hull.[40] Until 1833 the Hull Steam Packet Co. monopolised the Hull to London service but a rival firm, Hudson & Cobby, then commenced business. In 1835 this was taken over by the Humber Union Steam Co. and run by a committee of twelve proprietors. These included Henry Blundell, Joseph Jones, draper, John Parker, copper-smith, Francis Ullathorne, draper, and John Hudson, a druggist who was in partnership with Thomas Wilson, iron merchant and shipowner. The proprietors were mainly tradesmen or manufacturers with little experience in the trans-shipment of goods. By 1839 the company was in considerable debt and in 1841 was taken over by General Steam Navigation of London, the loss to the shareholders being estimated at £53,714. Another local enterprise, experiencing a similar fate, was the Hull Shipping Co.; this was established at the end of 1838, when there was a demand for first-rate vessels for the New York trade, but failed by September 1841.[41]

In the early 1830s the local firms were joined by the St. George Steam Packet Company of Dublin, which began steamship services between Hull and Gothenburg and Hull and Hamburg in 1834. The former was discontinued in the same year but re-opened by Wilson, Hudson & Co. in 1840. The Hamburg service was continued until 1842, when Gee & Co. of Hull, who had entered the Hamburg trade in 1836, took it over. The St. George Co. also participated in the Rotterdam trade and sent ships to Antwerp and Dunkirk in 1839, and Brownlow & Pearson (formerly Weddle & Brownlow) engaged actively in the Hamburg trade with regular services during the 1830s. Steamships owned by other non-local companies also frequented the port in the 1830s. These included the Aberdeen Steam Navigation Co., the Antwerp Steam Packet Co., the Liverpool and Glasgow S.S. Co., the Newcastle Steam Packet Co., the

---

[40] *H.A.* 1 Aug. 1823.
[41] H.B.C., D.M.B., 6 Sept. 1841.

Newcastle S.S. Co. and the Whitby Steam Packet Co. With the steamship still in its infancy, the sailing ship predominated especially in the overseas trade. In fact, in 1841 only 2,758 (or 3.8 per cent) of the total of 73,191 tons of shipping registered at Hull was propelled by steam and this was higher than the national average of 3.3 per cent. The expansion at Hull might have been accelerated had the Hull Dock Company adopted a more enlightened approach towards dock development; in 1837, when local steamship owners requested the Company to provide suitable accommodation for their vessels, some of which were too large to enter the lock gates, they were told to build their vessels to suit the capacity of the docks.[42]

The depression in shipping in the late 1820s, to which reference has already been made, reduced the demand for Hull-built ships. Between 1815 and 1822 about twelve Hull shipbuilders produced nearly 13,600 tons, with five of these firms accounting for nearly 70 per cent of the total output.[43] In 1823-6 nearly the same tonnage was built as in the previous eight years, but between 1827 and 1833 only 8,000 tons were built and registered at Hull. Most of the witnesses before the Select Committee on Manufactures, Commerce and Shipping in 1833 who represented the shipowning interests emphasised the depressed state of their industry. Edward Gibson, giving evidence, admitted that shipbuilding at Hull was being carried on only to employ apprentices and to use straight timber, unsuitable for repairs.

The Hull yards were affected by the decline in whaling, for part of the fleet had been locally built, but the local shipbuilders were also facing competition from other yards, especially at Sunderland. Between 1815 and 1832 Sunderland increased its share of U.K. shipbuilding tonnage from seventeen to 27 per cent. Declines in freights and competition from foreign shipowners also reduced the demand for ships from the Hull yards. Gibson, however, had been experimenting with steam vessel construction as early as 1828 and in 1834 built the 133-ton *Albatross*. He launched three others in 1835-7, one each for the Hull Steam Packet Co., Gee & Co. and the St. George Steam Packet Co. In 1837 Brownlow & Pearson launched the *Victoria* for the Hull Steam Packet Co. and, unlike those in the wooden steamship built by Edward Gibson in the same year which were not locally made, the engines and boilers in the *Victoria* were designed and constructed by the builders themselves. In the late 1830s, however, Hull shipbuilders shared in the increased demand for vessels which followed the rise in overseas trade and the known output from Hull yards in 1841 was almost as high as in the mid-1820 boom years. By 1841, also, shipping registered at Hull had risen to 73,200 tons, an increase of fifteen per cent since 1835.

* * *

While the investment in whaling had played an important role in Hull's economy in the early decades of the century, the justification for such an extensive commitment was already being questioned

---

[42] *H.A.* 28 Apr. 1837.
[43] These were Dikes & King, E. Gibson, the Gleadows, Steemson, and Walton.

by 1821. The *Hull Advertiser* drew the attention of its readers in December of that year to two vessels leaving Whitby with stores for the West Indian plantations and the hope was expressed that Hull merchants and shipowners would participate in this trade. It was argued that 'had part of the very extensive capital employed in the whale fishery been directed to this object some time ago, instead of that branch of our commerce being completely overdone and a large portion of the capital sunk, the town might have been in a very different state both as it [sic] regards the above classes and the inhabitants at large'. In the mid-1830s the local historian J. Greenwood reiterated this view in his *Picture of Hull* (1835) by expressing the opinion

> of many well-informed men, that the Greenland fishery has been greatly overdone and proved injurious to the general trade of this port, by withdrawing an undue proportion of capital from other branches of Commerce. The Mediterranean and Leghorn trade, from want of due cultivation, has here dwindled away into insignificance and the American trade, that rich source of wealth to Liverpool is in Hull of but limited extent. The West India trade has been attempted several times, but never established and two or three vessels have sailed hence to the East Indies, without as yet producing any profitable returns.

In the following year a correspondent to the *Hull Advertiser* of 9 September complained that

> not a ship ever arrives here from the West Indies; scarcely any from South America; none from the East Indies, none from Africa, the southern states of America or the Mauritius; in fine, nothing but timber, oil and one or two other staple articles, while a hundred are neglected if not despised. Why should not Hull have a flourishing West India trade?

These comments were re-echoed in 1840 when Thomas Wilson —iron merchant, shipowner and chairman of the Hull Chamber of Commerce (founded in 1837)—referred to those parts of the world in which Hull had no interest.[44] Of the East Indian trade 'how large a share fell to our lot he was ashamed to say',[45] and he mentioned Australia 'with which we had literally no connection', although British trade with Australia had in fact been increasing faster during the 1830s than total British exports. He referred in this context to the British trade with Sydney being a very extensive one, a large proportion of outward cargoes from London consisting of

> manufactured goods from our own immediate neighbourhood, whilst the homeward cargoes (principally wool) are re-shipped in London, to pass our very doors and to be consumed by places which ought to be dependent upon us. That a share of this trade might easily be obtained, he personally knew; and he could also vouch for its being a lucrative one.

---

[44] 3rd A.G.M. of the Hull Chamber of Commerce, 28 Feb. 1840.
[45] In 1838 a local merchant, Thomas Thompson, had sent a vessel to Calcutta: Eastern Morning News, *The Trade and Commerce of Hull and its Ships and Shipowners* (1878), p. 101.

He was reported as commenting on the port's transactions with North and South America as being 'so circumscribed as to be almost nugatory' and as recalling the time when regular trading vessels sailed from the port to

Genoa, Leghorn, Malta, Messina, Naples and Palermo but these have long ceased to exist; since that period an extensive commerce has been called into existence with Egypt, the Greek Islands, and the ports of the Black Sea; in none of which can it be fairly said that we partake. The Pacific Ocean, important as it is in a mercantile point of view, is to us a blank. To come nearer home, where is our trade with France, Portugal and Spain,[46] with the exception of the former country, and that to one particular port, all is gone—gone, as many other trades have done to Liverpool or to those who choose to take them . . . He would ask, ought these things so to be? And can a Chamber of Commerce be instrumental in bringing about a better state of things? He was of opinion that it could; the commerce he alluded to was mainly carried on by the enterprise of British merchants resident in the ports enjoying such commerce, and the thing required is to stimulate our own merchants to the same enterprise. United exertion can perform great things, where individuals would entirely fail.

Thomas Wilson was born in 1792 at Hull and had been trained as an iron merchant in the old-established firm of Wilkinson, Whitaker & Co. By 1824 he was trading on his own[47] and shortly afterwards was in partnership with J. Beckington, a Newcastle merchant. The partners were soon investing in shipping and in 1831 owned the *Swift*, of 100 tons, jointly with John Hudson, a Hull druggist, and Thomas Hudson, a gentleman of Newcastle. This ship had been built in County Durham and in the same year the firm acquired a Whitby-built vessel of 124 tons. Two years later Beckington, Wilson & Co. was permitted a £3,000 discount account with the Bank of England, and Wilson's capital was stated to be £20,000. In 1835 the partnership was dissolved but for the next few years Thomas Wilson traded with the Hudsons, as Wilson, Hudson & Co., and by 1840 the firm had a fleet of six ships and was acting as agents for the Berwick Steam Packet Co. and the St. George Steam Packet Co. In 1841 the firm was renamed Thomas Wilson, Sons & Co., the founder having been joined by his sons Arthur, Charles and David, and played a major role in the subsequent trade and shipping history of Hull.

There was clearly some justification for the contemporary criticisms that undue emphasis had been placed on whale fishing to the detriment of investment in widening the trade connections of the port. Comparatively little had been done to extend the sphere of the port's trading activities beyond Northern Europe, except for the

---

[46] In 1840 inward tonnages from these countries were only three per cent of total inward tonnages from overseas.

[47] In an account book believed to have belonged to John Hudson is an entry in the name of Thomas Wilson, dating from 1824 and including transactions in iron: Kingston upon Hull Record Office, Guildhall: DBX 1/1.

enforced shipments of wood from British North America; the proximity of markets in Northern Europe probably engendered complacency among the mercantile community. When cotton manufacture began in 1838, providing employment especially for Hull's female population, a suggestion was made that further opportunities for male employment might be obtained 'by the formation of joint stock shipping companies than which (sic) no port is so well situated as is abundantly proved by the great number of north-country and foreign vessels annually resorting to it to supply the deficiency in our own shipping'.[48] That some such attempts, made in the late 1830s, had ended in failure has already been shown and there was much evidence of inexperienced persons involving themselves in joint stock companies without much success. It was especially those merchants whose own trading activities were speculative who invested in such enterprises and who were largely dependent upon bank finance to meet their obligations.

The spirit of optimism which pervaded the Hull mercantile community in the mid-1830s, with the general improvement in the economic climate, was vividly epitomised in 1836 by Henry Broadley when he said that

> he did think the tide of prosperity was setting favourably for this town and they had nothing at all to do but patiently to ride upon it. They knew that our great bard, who had said everything better than anyone else, had stated—'There is a tide in the affairs of men, if taken at the flood leads on to fortune'. On such a flood we were in Hull now embarked and we must take the current whilst it serves, or lose our adventure.[49]

But in the late 1830s the port's economy was on the eve of increased competition and it was essential that further initiative be exerted if Hull were to maintain its place among Britain's major ports. It was not sufficient, as Henry Broadley had suggested, for the town 'to ride upon the tide of prosperity' and do nothing. Thomas Wilson had realised this and he and his family were to influence substantially the trading economy of the port in the second half of the 19th century.

[48] *H.A.* 23 Mar. 1838.
[49] *H.A.* 2 Sept. 1836.

III

1841-74

The rapid rise in inward tonnages at Hull during the second half of the 1830s raised the general volume of trading activities to a level at least 75 per cent higher than during the depressed years of the late 1820s and early 1830s. By 1844 the tonnage frequenting the port had surpassed previous levels and the average tonnages entering Hull during the 1840s were ten per cent above those of 1840. The port was, however, affected by the depressed state of the British economy in 1847-8 and this was reflected in a levelling-off in the rate of growth. In fact, the total volume of shipping frequenting the port remained almost static in the late 1840s and early 1850s and there is some evidence, although difficult to quantify, that Grimsby, on the south bank of the Humber, was beginning to develop into a more effective competitor to Hull.

In 1848 the Manchester, Sheffield and Lincolnshire Railway Co. opened a line to Grimsby and in 1852 the Royal Dock at Grimsby was completed. The Hull Dock Company admitted in its Annual Report for 1850 that whereas the trade of the ports of Goole, Grimsby and Gainsborough had greatly increased, that of Hull 'has been nearly stationary for the last five years'. In the early 1840s exports from Hull were, by value, about the same as those from London and in 1842 exceeded those of the latter port, but by the early 1850s Hull's share of the national export trade had declined whereas the share of goods shipped from London had increased. Hull suffered to some extent from its very high concentration on North European markets, since the growth in exports to these countries was less than to other areas (see Diagram I). Nevertheless, too much must not be made of the disadvantages of Hull's location, since Newcastle, also on the east coast, had higher export values in 1850 than ten years earlier although it had also the advantage of an expanding trade in coal exports.

Local opinion in the early 1850s, led by Henry Blundell, agitated for reductions in dock dues to counter competition from other east-coast ports. Four organisations were entitled to charges on the shipping of the port—the Commissioners of Pilots, Hull Corporation, Hull Dock Company and the Trinity House. In October 1850, in an attempt to ease the situation, the Dock Company sought the co-operation of Hull Corporation and the Trinity House. The Chamber of Commerce, at the outset of the agitation, circulated an address to some thousands of Hull ratepayers outlining their views on the subject. A committee of 50, with Henry Blundell as chairman, promoted the Dock Dues Bill and members included not only prominent merchants and shipowners but also shopkeepers. The Bill became law in 1852 and resulted in Hull Corporation abolishing its water-bailiff dues, while the Trinity House reduced its primage outwards by two-thirds and inwards by one-third, and reductions of 20 to 40 per cent were made by the Dock Company in its dues. During the evidence before a Select Committee on the Bill the absence of return cargoes for the ships bringing imports to Hull was cited as a factor in the port's trading difficulties. It was said that 'numerous vessels in which cargoes have been imported into this port sail from thence in ballast to Newcastle and other Northern ports and there load coals, coke and other goods for exportation to foreign parts'.[50]

Part of the trouble, therefore, may have been the failure at this period to develop the export trade in coal and for this the absence of a direct rail link between Hull and the Yorkshire coalfield could be held responsible. An attempt was made in 1845 to provide such a link by the promotion of a railway between Hull and Barnsley, but this failed in the following year.[51] The Hull and Selby Railway was leased in 1845 to the York and North Midland Railway, which became part of the North Eastern Railway Co. on the latter's formation in 1854, and it was not until 1869 that the latter company opened a line between Hull and Doncaster. This loss of control over the rail connections from Hull to the rest of the country, which made the port dependent until the 1880s on the policies of a company with other port connections (at Hartlepool for example), was a cause of constant complaint during subsequent decades.

With Hull's imports consisting primarily of raw materials and its exports mainly of manufactured goods, it was not surprising that the declared value of exports passing through the port exceeded that of its imports. In 1857, for example, exports (at £15.7 mill.) were twice imports (estimated at £7.8 mill.),[52] but by 1872, when the first total value data for imports at individual ports were published, the margin between the two had narrowed (£23.0 mill. exports, £16.5 mill. imports). In 1857 imports at Hull were only about 4.2 per cent of total British imports, whereas in the same year the port handled 12.9 per cent of British exports; fifteen years later its imports were 4.7 per cent of the U.K. total but its exports had declined to 9.0 per cent.

Exports from Hull continued to reflect the predominance of textiles in the British export trade of the mid 19th century. In 1850 cotton yarns and manufactures accounted for over half of the total value of goods exported (see Table IV) and woollen yarns and manufactures for over a quarter; linen yarns and manufactures, hardware, machinery and metals were the other main items. Hull was still one of the chief outlets for shipments of British cotton, linen and woollen yarns and over a third of British machinery exports left the port, but during the 1860s the competitive effect of the growth of Goole and Grimsby on Hull's export trade was apparent. Between 1860 and 1870 Grimsby's exports of British manufactures rose from £0.8 mill. to £12.2 mill. and at Goole from £0.3 mill. to £1.2 mill., an increase of £12.3 mill. for the two ports, whereas at Hull exports declined from 90 per cent of the Humber

[50] S.C. on the Kingston upon Hull Dock and Dues Bill (1852) MS.: H.U.L. DTR/4/45, p. 33.
[51] P.R.O. BT 41/840/4828.
[52] This estimate was obtained by taking the average values of the commodities imported into the U.K. and applying these to the quantities imported at Hull, detailed value analyses for individual ports not being available before 1895.

total in the late 1850s to 56 per cent ten years later. Expressed in national terms, thirteen of the fourteen per cent of British exports shipped from the Humber ports in 1857 was sent from Hull but during the 1860s, when Northern European countries increased their share of British exports (see Diagram I), it was the newer Humber ports which handled much of this traffic. In 1870 Hull accounted for only nine of the fifteen per cent of British exports shipped from the Humber (see Table IV), a state of affairs which justified the comment that the progress of Hull was not commensurate with the facilities for its extension.[53]

Coal exports especially had been retarded and after 1865 an absolute decline in this trade occurred, from 203,000 tons in that year to 172,000 tons in 1869; in contrast, coal exported from Grimsby rose by about 50,000 tons in the same period, from 172,000 to 220,000, and thus exceeded the coal trade of Hull. Hull's share in the Humber coal traffic had declined from about 70 per cent in 1860 to about 40 per cent by 1869, when the long-awaited link between the port and the coalfield area materialised with the opening of the railway to Doncaster.

It seems likely that transport facilities and the rates charged for the carriage of goods were important factors influencing the pattern of the Humber export trade. An arrangement was made in 1855 which regulated the rail traffic between the Lancashire and Yorkshire Railway, the North Eastern Railway and the Manchester, Sheffield and Lincolnshire Railway. Known as the Humber Agreement, this divided the receipts from goods traffic between the various lines on fixed ratios irrespective of the volume of traffic carried.[54] From 1 January 1855, 55 per cent of the revenue from this traffic was allocated to the Lancashire and Yorkshire and the North Eastern Railway and 45 per cent to the Manchester, Sheffield and Lincolnshire, and in 1860 the ratios were changed to 50 per cent to the two former lines and 50 per cent to the latter. As the Manchester, Sheffield and Lincolnshire Railway served Grimsby and the Lancashire and Yorkshire Railway had a line to Goole, there was clearly a practical inducement to ship increased quantities of goods from these ports. In addition, the North Eastern Railway, which owned the Hartlepool docks, encouraged trade to that port by the application of discriminatory charges. The same rates were charged from Hartlepool to the manufacturing districts as from Hull to these areas, although the distances from Hull were considerably less. In 1865 the North Eastern Railway Company and representatives from Hull Corporation, the Chamber of Commerce, local steamship owners and the Hull Dock Company discussed the possible transfer of the docks to the railway company. This was welcomed by the steamship owners but not by Hull Corporation and a public meeting was then called to consider the vesting of the docks in a trust. This proposal was submitted for parliamentary approval but, owing to

---

[53] Hull Chamber of Commerce, *General Price Current* (1870).
[54] Minutes of first meeting of representatives of the North Eastern, Lancashire and Yorkshire, and Manchester, Sheffield and Lincolnshire Railways, 7 June 1855: British Railways Archives, York.

opposition from ratepayers, the Dock Company and the railway, it failed to pass a House of Commons committee.[55]

In the 1850s and 1860s Hull's import trade was still primarily concerned with raw materials—flax, grains, especially wheat and barley, hemp, iron ore, oilseeds, wood and wool. Wheat imports fluctuated widely in the years between 1840 and 1870, the high level of 1839 being exceeded only in 1862 and 1867. In the early years the wheat came mainly through Prussian ports but by 1867 the bulk came from Odessa, the Danube and Egypt, with smaller quantities from Australia, California and Chile. In the early 1860s and towards the end of that decade the U.S.A. became Britain's major source, but as Hull had few trading connections with America at this period its share of national imports declined, from eight per cent in 1857 to two per cent in 1870. Up to the latter date the flour-milling industry at Hull, as elsewhere, was still traditional in organisation and quite small in scale. Steam power was installed at the Hull Anti-Mill in 1848 and by 1851 several more of the port's 23 flour mills were converted to steam. Included among Hull's flour millers at mid-century was James Rank. His father John, an East Riding miller, had migrated to Hull in the early 1840s and started at a mill in Holderness Road, where about half the town's flour mills were located. During the 1860s some of the older millers had closed down and the industry was on the threshold of a new era. A partial roller system was introduced in Britain in this decade but it was not until late in the 1870s that the first complete roller system, without the traditional mill-stones, was built; so far as can be ascertained Hull's first roller plant was installed in 1884.

With its emphasis on European trade, the port was vulnerable to the effects of the Crimean War but the slump in shipping tonnage in the years 1854-5 was less severe than expected. The frontiers of Prussia remained open for the transport of goods to and from Russia and this enabled flax, hemp, tallow and linseed, which could bear the land transport charges from Memel and Königsberg, to be exported and, except for linseed, imports from Russia were adequate for local consumption. Output contracted at the local oil mills; in 1855 not more than three or four of the 27 mills were working. Some supplies of seed were obtained coastwise from London having been landed there from India, and a few cargoes from the Mediterranean were shipped direct to Hull.

In 1856 overseas trade expanded rapidly and over one million tons of shipping frequented the Hull docks. Imports in that year included 500,000 quarters of linseed—the highest quantity up to that time. By the mid-1850s Hull had become Britain's primary seed-crushing centre and the original stamper presses were being replaced by hydraulic machinery. Some of these were obtained locally from the Old Foundry, now under the proprietorship of Christiana Rose, daughter of Duncan Campbell, one of the earlier partners. In 1858 Alexander Samuelson, the brother and partner of

---

[55] W. W. Tomlinson, *The North Eastern Railway: its rise and development* (1914), p. 623.

Martin Samuelson, a Hull engineer and shipbuilder, stated in a paper to the Institution of Mechanical Engineers that 'to crush the seed imported in 1856 there were required about 150 to 160 double hydraulic presses at work day and night; nearly 100 of these are at work in Hull and the rest are distributed all over the country, the important mills being in London, Liverpool, Grimsby etc.'[56]

The oilseed trade accounted for about a fifth of the estimated total value of all goods imported at Hull in 1857 (see Table V) and nearly half the U.K. linseed imports were shipped to Hull and processed in the local mills. When, in 1864, cotton seed was imported at Hull for the first time, the Hull Chamber of Commerce's publication *The General Price Current* estimated that this raw material employed 'probably one fifth of the crushing power of the port'. The inauguration of this traffic was an important contributory factor in the growth of seed-crushing in Hull. New mills were built and the number of firms rose from 25 in 1861 to 37 in 1872 and 40 in 1876—probably the highest number at any one time. Grain imports were of about the same value as the oilseed trade in 1857 and taken together these raw materials accounted for about 40 per cent of the estimated value of Hull's import trade in that year. Cattle bones were still being imported and, although the quantities had declined to about half the volume of the 1830s (averaging 14,000 tons in the 1850s and 1860s), Hull was handling sixteen per cent of U.K. imports in 1857. The port also participated in the guano trade, especially in the 1860s. In 1865 21,000 tons of this commodity, which came mainly from Peru, was handled at Hull and, like the bone dust, was used for manure. Hull's share of the national trade in guano was nine per cent in that year but ten years later it was handling only three per cent of the British imports. The bone trade declined rapidly in the 1880s and was negligible by the end of the century.

Flax and hemp accounted for twelve per cent of all imports but the extent of their local utilisation is not known. Hull's cotton industry had been enlarged in 1845 when the Kingston Cotton Mill Co. was established, spinning operations commencing in 1848. Like the Hull Flax and Cotton Mill Co., it had a somewhat chequered career and in the early 1860s, when the American Civil War restricted cotton supplies and the price of raw cotton rose, both mills were closed for a time. In 1860, before the war started, nearly 45 per cent of U.K. re-exports of raw cotton were shipped from Hull but in 1862 this proportion had declined to 27 per cent, although the port had almost regained its earlier share of this trade by 1870. Cotton manufacture at the first of the Hull mills had ceased by the mid-1870s but the Kingston Company continued until 1894.

The failure of these companies was due to their inability to accumulate adequate reserves with which to modernise their machinery and withstand periods of severe trade depression. This situation arose principally from inefficient management, due mainly

---

[56] A. Samuelson, 'On Oil Mill Machinery', *Proceedings of the Institution of Mechanical Engineers* (1858), p. 38.

to the inexperience of almost all the directors and shareholders, who thus became dependent upon single individuals for managing the mills.[57] The Hull cotton industry, originally established by members of the mercantile community anxious to benefit from the increased demand for British cotton goods—as indicated by the volume of cotton products shipped from the port—was important in Hull's mid-century economy, but its impact on the trade and shipping of Hull does not appear to have been large. In the 1840s at least eight large sailing vessels, of between 502 and 802 tons and owned by Joseph Rylands, manager of the Hull Flax and Cotton Mill Co., were registered at the port. They brought cargoes of cotton to Hull but this was only a temporary development, for Rylands died in 1854 and the quantity of raw cotton imported at Hull was less than one per cent of the U.K. total from 1857 until the mid-1880s.[58]

Wood imports accounted for about a fifth of the trade tonnage of the port in 1843[59] but in value terms were only six per cent of the 1857 estimate. It was undoubtedly the requirements of this trade which led to the building of Victoria Dock, of twelve and a half acres, opened in 1850; the seasonal arrival of wood cargoes had previously caused much dock congestion. At a public meeting convened to discuss dock accommodation in 1836, a Hull timber merchant stated that as many as 20 vessels were in the port at a time and as each of them was expected to deliver from 80 to 100 pieces a day 'it is quite impossible for 1,500 or 1,600 pieces of timber in one day to pass out of our docks into the Old Harbour where the timber yards are chiefly'.[60] Competition from Grimsby and especially from Hartlepool was experienced in the late 1850s and during the 1860s, when the North Eastern Railway's unequal rates, to which reference has been made, caused some wood imports to be diverted from Hull to Hartlepool. Merchants were able to ship their supplies to the latter port at lower sea freights and also benefit from the lower landing charges there. But for these factors, wood imports at Hull might have been substantially higher; even so, by 1863, when an extension of Victoria Dock by eight acres was completed, they had exceeded previous levels and a steady upward trend was maintained to 1868. This coincided with a growth in local house and other building and a general upsurge of industrial activity in the British economy.

Between 1861 and 1876 the number of Hull timber merchants more than doubled, from 20 to 44, and of the latter number twelve also engaged in saw-milling. A decline in the supply of native-grown larch and fir created a rising demand for foreign timber and in the early 1870s hewn timber imports at Hull included large quantities of mining timber and pit props from Norway and Sweden. About 1860 Hockney & Liggins, local joiners, began to

[57] See Joyce M. Bellamy, 'Cotton Manufacture in . . . Hull', *Business History*, vol. iv, no. 2 (1962), pp. 91-108.
[58] The only data so far located on cotton imports at Hull before 1857 are for 1840-3 and these are not comparable with the later figures.
[59] J. B. Hartley, *Report . . . with reference to the proposed extension of the dock accommodation of the Port of Hull* (1843), pp. 4-6.
[60] *H.A.* 9 Sept. 1836.

manufacture wood products for builders and joiners by using steam power and were pioneers of an industry which became increasingly important in later decades. Population growth, which was considerable during the 1860s and 1870s, increased the demand for housing and industrial buildings, thus providing further stimuli for the wood trade of the port. From 101,185 in 1861, the population rose by 25 per cent to 125,943 in 1871 and in the next ten years there was an increase of 32 per cent to 165,974.

The main change in the pattern of inward traffic at Hull between 1840 and 1870 was the decline in the trade with the British North American colonies, from fourteen per cent to two per cent, due to the relaxation of the timber duties in the 1840s and their final abolition in 1866. The increased tonnages from Africa reflected the growing trade with Egypt in wheat and cotton seed. Overall the volume of traffic both inwards and outwards had risen substantially in the middle decades of the century. Nevertheless there is some evidence that much of Hull's traditional export traffic was being affected by inter-port competition, for its shares of U.K. exports of cotton yarns and manufactures, linen yarn and woollen and worsted yarns and manufactures declined substantially between 1850 and 1870 (see Table IV). A rapid expansion in British overseas trade from the late 1860s to 1872, however, was reflected at Hull in a rise in inward and outward traffic which placed a considerable strain on the dock and rail facilities of the port. Terminal accommodation proved inadequate, the Hull rail sidings were blocked with wagons, and vessels were unable to receive or discharge their cargoes.

During the early 1870s there was much discussion of new schemes for improvement. Proposals for a tunnel to take a railway under the Humber were submitted in 1871 but this scheme, which passed a House of Commons committee in 1873, was rejected by the House of Lords.[61] Factors which may have influenced their lordships probably included a North Eastern Railway offer to grant full running powers to the Manchester, Sheffield and Lincolnshire Railway on the North Eastern's lines to Hull, although Charles Wilson had emphasised that running powers were useless if the line were blocked. Criticism of the dock facilities as well as technical difficulties may also have determined the adverse decision. At the time the promoters of the railway Bill believed that, by means of the North Eastern Railway's offer, they had obtained additional railway facilities by a more rapid method than their own scheme, but their satisfaction was short-lived. In 1875, when the North Eastern Railway, by an agreement with the Lancashire and Yorkshire Railway, obtained access to goods stations and docks at Goole[62] trade from the latter port increased.

*　*　*

---

[61] The House of Lords Committee recorded that the preamble to the Bill was not proved but no reasons for the decision were given in the MS. minutes of evidence: H. of L. records, 21 July 1873.

[62] Agreement between the North Eastern Railway and the Lancashire and Yorkshire Railway, 17 June 1875: British Railways Archives, York.

Whaling on a smaller scale than before was revived at Hull in the 1840s in conjunction with seal-catching but, by the middle of the decade, Peterhead in Scotland 'had clearly displaced Hull as Britain's leading whaling port'.[63] The ships sent from Dundee also increased, the trade being stimulated there by a demand from the local jute industry for whale oil. Larger ships were used and the Scottish ports' proximity to the fishing grounds enabled sealing in the spring off Greenland or Newfoundland to be combined with a whaling season in the summer in the Davis Straits. At Hull during the 1850s and 1860s the maximum number of ships to return in any one year was fourteen. In 1857 the *Diana*, which sailed from Hull in the 1840s and early 1850s, was equipped with steam propulsion by the local shipowners, Brown, Atkinson & Co. In 1860 the Whale and Seal Fishery Co. Ltd. was formed to extend this trade; this company was liquidated after a few years and another one, the Hull Fishing Co. Ltd., was created. By 1865 just over half of its authorised capital of £9,000 had been subscribed. From its predecessor the new company took over the *Diana* and a sailing ship, the *Truelove*. Brown, Atkinson & Co. were among the principal proprietors, who also included some of the local merchants and other businessmen,[64] but the venture was not a success and the *Truelove* was withdrawn. When the *Diana* was lost on a homeward voyage in 1869, whale fishing from Hull ceased. A new element in the trade and shipping of the port had, however, emerged with the introduction of trawl-fishing.

Trawling smacks from Devon and Kent were fishing in the North Sea in the 1830s, with Hull and Scarborough being used as summer trawling stations, but contemporary evidence suggests that it was not until the mid-1840s that the trade became established at Hull.[65] The number of smacks sailing from Hull for the North Sea fishing grounds in 1854 has been variously put at 21, 29 and 40. Unlike the whalers, the tonnage of which usually exceeded 200, the boats which pioneered the Hull fishing industry were sailing vessels of under 50 registered tons. Their owners were individual entrepreneurs who frequently depended on mortgages to finance their craft. Most of these early vessels were built in Essex, Devon and Kent, but some came from Hull and Grimsby shipyards. In the late 1840s R. Vivian, from Cornwall, registered five fishing smacks at Hull and other smack-owners came to Hull from Ramsgate and Devon. In 1851 just over 1,000 persons from Cornwall, Devon and Kent were living in Hull.

Further expansion of trawling occurred in the fifties, when Robert Hellyer, of Brixham, among others, settled in Hull. Up to this time the facilities for the trade were meagre, the fish being landed near Nelson Street, adjacent to the ferry-boat pier. In the mid-1850s,

---

[63] S. G. E. Lythe, 'The Dundee Whale Fishery', *Scottish Journal of Political Economy*, vol. xi (1964), p. 163.

[64] These included Joseph Blundell, seed-crusher, C. & W. Earle and W. Gibson, shipbuilders, Thomas Holmes and T. B. Holmes, tanners, T. Shipham, brassfounder and J. H. Ellerman, merchant.

[65] See Joyce M. Bellamy, 'Pioneers of the Hull Trawl Fishing Industry', *The Mariner's Mirror*, vol. li, no. 2 (1965), pp. 185-7.

when some smack-owners left Hull for Grimsby, where the fish trade was being encouraged, the Hull Dock Company provided shed accommodation on the south-west quay of Humber Dock, where a daily fish market was held. Much of the fish traffic by-passed Hull, however, and was sent direct from the fishing grounds to the London market by fast sailing cutters. The railway companies then reduced the carriage rates for fish to the metropolis and manufacturing districts in the 1850s and the tonnage of fish landed at Hull rose from 1,571 tons in 1854 to 10,782 tons ten years later.[66] With 260 smacks using the port in 1867, when only five vessels (a quarter of the daily arrivals) could be berthed at a time compared with 50 at Grimsby, Hull smack-owners pressed for improved facilities. Shipping entering the port from the fishing grounds rose from 86,100 tons to 143,600 tons between 1861 and 1868, but half the catch went direct to London. In 1869, when the smack-owners, after protracted negotiations, were permitted to use the newly-opened Albert Dock, of 24½ acres, about 1,200 men were regularly sailing from Hull. Some thousands more were employed in ancillary trades as packers, labourers, carters, coopers, sail-makers, smiths, painters, ship- and boat-builders, twine-spinners, and block- and rope-makers. By 1873 some 330 smacks frequented the port and trawl-fishing had become a well-established sector in Hull's economy.

★   ★   ★

During the 1840s Hull's steam shipping services were extended with regular sailings to Bremen and Antwerp from 1844 and to St. Petersburg from 1845. By 1851 twelve per cent of Hull's registered tonnage of 59,166 tons was powered by steam engines; almost all the ships were locally owned, the main firms being Brownlow, Pearson & Co., the Hull Steam Packet Co.[67] and Joseph Gee, which between them accounted for about three-quarters of the Hull steamship tonnage in the forties. Other owners included C. L. Ringrose, Thomas Wilson and a few smaller firms. Ships of the Hanseatic Steam Packet Co., the Elbe and Humber Steam Navigation Co. and the North of Europe Steam Navigation Co. also frequented the port.

Only a few of the locally owned steamships had, at that time, been built at Hull. In the early 1850s, however, two engineering firms, C. & W. Earle and Martin Samuelson, began to build iron steamships, although Samuelson also built sailing vessels and most of his customers were non-local. At about the same time, Thomas Wilson, Sons & Co. were extending their interest in shipping activities. In 1853 the firm had a capital of £40,000 and was allowed a £15,000 discount account with the Bank of England. Between 1854 and 1871 the Wilsons acquired 55 ships, of which 39 were built by C. & W. Earle and included vessels varying in size from about 500

---

[66] *H. & E.C.H.* 25 Nov. 1869.
[67] The activities of this company appear to have ceased in the early 1860s, ships owned by it having been either sold or broken up at that time: Custom House Hull, Registry of Ships.

tons, built in the 1850s, to 1,800 tons, built in 1871.[68] In the 1850s and early 1860s the Wilson ships traded mainly with Baltic and other North European ports but in the sixties some of their ships went to the Mediterranean. By 1860, when David, one of Thomas's three sons, withdrew from the firm, the capital had risen to £70,000. Thomas retired in 1867 and died two years later but Charles and Arthur Wilson continued the business, and when the Franco-German War of 1870 closed the Prussian Baltic ports the firm started a regular service to Trieste. After the opening of the Suez Canal in 1869, the Wilsons inaugurated a fleet of steamers for a service between London, Colombo, Madras and Calcutta. This was so successful that vessels of over 3,000 tons register, some of them from Earle's, were obtained in 1873.

Another prominent firm of shipowners was Bailey & Leetham, established about 1856 by a ship broker and two former sea captains. In the years before 1871 only four of its fleet of 28 vessels were built by Earle's, but six came from the yards of two other Hull builders, Gilbert & Cooper and Humphrys & Pearson. The latter firm was established about 1869 by J. Humphrys and F. H. Pearson (son of William Pearson of Brownlow & Co.), the opening of the Suez Canal having stimulated the demand for steamships. A ship of 1,200 tons was launched in 1869 for Bailey & Leetham, who undertook the mail service between Lisbon and the west coast of Africa, although their vessels mainly traded with European ports. Among the smaller steamship owners the old firm of W. & C. L. Ringrose was still in business, engaging mainly in the Dutch trade, and Smith, Hill & Co., established in the 1860s, had concentrated mainly on the Mediterranean and Montreal trades.

From the 1840s to early 1870s shipping registered at Hull increased by about 100,000 tons but the growth rate was uneven. It was comparatively static in the fifties and early sixties, but a rapid expansion occurred in the years 1864-74—from 72,000 tons to 175,000 tons—and due entirely to an expansion in the tonnage of steamships registered at the port. In 1867 steam shipping registered at Hull totalled 46,490 tons and surpassed, for the first time, the registered sailing tonnage of the port, which was 44,593. Hull's growth rate in this respect exceeded the national level and rose from four per cent of U.K. steamship tonnage in 1864 to 9.3 per cent in 1871. This absolute and relative growth in Hull's steam shipping trade was probably due to the port's pre-occupation with the short-distance European traffic in which the steamship predominated.[69] But it was also due to the co-operation between local shipowners and builders and especially to the enterprise of T. Wilson, Sons & Co. By the early 1870s regular steamship services linked Hull to all the principal European ports and connections with more remote parts of the world were being developed.

---

[68] In 1871 Earle's Shipbuilding & Engineering Co. Ltd., a public company, was formed to take over the business formerly carried on by C. & W. Earle. See Joyce M. Bellamy, 'A Hull Shipbuilding Firm', *Business History*, vol. vi, no. 1 (1963), for the history of this firm.

[69] G. S. Graham, 'The Ascendancy of the Sailing Ship, 1850-85', *Economic History Review*, 2nd ser., vol. ix (1956-7), no. 1, p. 81.

IV

1875-1900

Following the boom years of the early 1870s, Hull's mercantile activities reflected the generally depressed economic climate prevailing throughout the country in the later years of the decade. There is, moreover, some evidence that Hull was declining relatively in its share of both inward and outward cargoes. Some eighteen per cent of shipping clearing from Hull left the port in ballast in 1877— the highest proportion for at least 24 years, the figure for 1853 being 22 per cent. Whereas at Bristol, Glasgow, Goole and Harwich the values of British exports had risen, at Hull they had decreased. Competition from Goole, Harwich and Newcastle in imports was also influencing the trade at Hull where, in only one of its major commodities, imported wheat, was there an absolute and relative increase in its trade.

One of the major trade developments of the last years of the century was a growth in coal exports from Hull but in the late 1870s it was this trade which aroused the greatest anxiety, for after 1874 an absolute decline in the quantity shipped from Hull had occurred— from 507,000 tons in 1874 to 413,000 tons in 1879—whereas shipments from Goole rose from 137,000 tons to 243,000 tons. Hull's share of the Humber coal traffic declined during these years from 53 to 45 per cent. A letter from South Yorkshire coal-owners to Charles Wilson in February 1879[70] highlights the reasons for the stagnation in the trade:

> Owing to the continued depression in trade, the coalowners are again compelled to seek for a reduction of the high rate of carriage and charges for shipping coal, and as a director of both the railway and Dock Company we beg to solicit your influence to further this object. As a large shipowner no one is in a better position than yourself to see and know practically the effect of disproportionate rates and charges such as are made at Hull in comparison with competing ports. October 1st 1872, the rate on coal from the Barnsley district to Hull was advanced 6d. per ton and July 1st 1876, it was reduced 4d., so we are still charged 2d. more per ton than before, although coal is now selling at less than half the price it was and rails, timber and all other railway materials have fallen considerably. Under these circumstances it is surely not too much to ask the railway companies to assist their customers to maintain their business by reducing the rate to meet the altered times. We have never yet been able to understand why our coal should be charged 3s. 2d. per ton; while coal is carried from Normanton, a further distance than some of our collieries at 2s. 3d. If the latter can be worked to pay, and no doubt it does, are we not in South Yorkshire altogether overrated. As to shipping coal at Hull, we need hardly say that while the facilities are far behind those of Grimsby or Goole, the Dock Company's charges are consider-

---

[70] *M. of P.*, H. of L., Hull and Barnsley Railway and Dock Bill, 1880, Q. 295.

ably more. For instance, at Hull we have to pay 3d. to 7d. per ton, while the cost at Grimsby is uniform, say 2d. per ton and at Goole 6d. per 5 tons and no restriction made as to the build of wagons. We have frequently urged the subject of rates and charges upon both railway and dock companies but regret that it does not appear to have received such consideration as we think its importance deserves. If your trade is to be maintained it is absolutely necessary that the carriage rate and shipping charges should be revised at once, otherwise we shall see it taken to other and more favoured districts which are now competing with us for orders in foreign markets.

Following this letter the Hull Dock Company met the board of the North Eastern Railway, which declined to reduce its rates. Local agitation among the business community then led to the promotion of a Bill for a new railway and dock. A committee, including local shipowners, merchants, industrialists and some colliery owners,[71] was formed in May 1879 for this purpose and, rather ironically, from 1 July 1879 the North Eastern Railway reduced the coal carriage rates to Hull. This provides yet another example in the port's history of improvements obtained following pressure by members of the mercantile community. In 1880 coal exports from Hull rose to 601,000 tons, thus exceeding previous levels. In that year, however, Charles Wilson had warned members of the Chamber of Commerce of the dangers facing Hull unless the Hull and Barnsley Railway scheme was achieved: 'at present nearly every competing port has a connection of railway and dock interests and when we see Harwich taking away business that used to come to the Humber in consequence of the connection of the railway, dock and steam interest,[72] we are shown that unless very decisive measures are adopted to put an end to the unfair competition not only in that quarter but others, our trade will gradually diminish'. The Hull, Barnsley and West Riding Junction Railway and Dock Bill passed the House of Commons committee in July 1880 and the need for improved dock facilities was emphasised by witnesses before the House of Lords committee. Alderman C. Wells, a Hull coal merchant who was also a colliery proprietor, indicated that the quay space was deficient, a point raised during the 1873 attempt to obtain improved rail facilities. He also emphasised the need of greater depth of water for the Californian grain ships and the large Wilson liners, which had to discharge their cargoes into lighters in the Humber owing to insufficient depth of water in Victoria Dock. Eight of the Wilson

---

[71] Members of the committee were Dr. King, the Mayor; Col. Brooshooft, landowner; H. Briggs, shipowner; W. Day, colliery proprietor; A. Eggington, banker; J. S. Eggington, landowner; W. Field, merchant; J. Fisher, timber merchant; H. Hodge, seed-crusher; E. Leetham, shipowner; W. Massey, shipowner and coal merchant; J. P. Pope, colliery proprietor; W. Rayment, ship chandler; F. Reckitt, merchant and manufacturer; L. Stephenson, silk mercer; J. Stuart, seed-crusher; J. C. Thompson, engineer; C. Wells, coal merchant and shipowner; G. Whitehead, engineer and forge owner; R. Willows, silk mercer; and W. E. Woolf, shipowner and coal merchant.

[72] Served by the Great Central Railway, much traffic was sent from the West Riding direct to Harwich.

ships had been grounded, involving considerable expense in repairs, and ships requiring dry docking were sent to Grimsby, owing to inadequate graving facilities at Hull. The Bill received the Royal Assent on 18 October 1880.

Also in 1880 the Hull Dock Company had opened William Wright Dock, of nearly six acres, and in 1883 the Company's St. Andrew's Dock, of ten and a half acres, was completed. The latter was allocated to the fishing trade, the expansion of which had necessitated further accommodation. Between 1880 and 1885 the tonnages of shipping entering the port from America had declined and the difficulties which steamship owners at Hull had experienced were emphasised by Charles Wilson, when he said in 1881 at a meeting of the Chamber of Commerce that

> the charges at Hull are so high in comparison with other ports, the extra distance is so great and the navigation of the Humber seems becoming so dangerous that it is really an impossibility for large modern steamships to come to Hull and be employed regularly in the American trade at present. We have brought the case strongly before the Hull Dock Company but they say they are so short of money that they cannot see their way clear to do anything.[73]

It was therefore not until the opening in July 1885 of the Hull and Barnsley Company's Alexandra Dock, of 46 acres, which provided deep-water berths for the larger merchant ships and special facilities for coal traffic, that any major increase in the water area of Hull docks for general trading was obtained. The independent railway line, which ran between Hull and the Barnsley area and was also owned by the Company, was opened in the same month.

Finance for this ambitious scheme, which had an authorised share capital of £3 mill. and borrowing powers up to £2.5 mill., had been subscribed by a number of local shareholders, including Hull Corporation, but many were also located outside the area and most of the debenture stock was held by non-local owners.[74] The opening of the new railway and dock was followed by an intensive rate war between the new company, the North Eastern Railway and the Hull Dock Company, and the years between 1885 and 1893, when the North Eastern Railway Company took over the Hull Dock Company, were fraught with financial difficulties for both the new company and the old one.[75]

The Act (56 and 57 Vic.) which permitted the amalgamation of the North Eastern Railway and the Hull Dock Company prohibited the Company from reducing the dock dues below those of the Hull and Barnsley, except by agreement. The North Eastern, moreover, was not allowed to build a dock eastward of the River Hull without giving notice to the Hull and Barnsley Company, which could require it to be built as a joint undertaking. This arrangement was

---

[73] A.G.M., Hull Chamber of Commerce, 10 Nov. 1881.
[74] Proprietors' Address Books 1887 and 1889 and List of Debenture Holders (n.d.), Kingston upon Hull Record Office, Guildhall. The largest debenture holders lived in London.
[75] See Tomlinson, *The N.E. Railway*, pp. 707-715.

distrusted by Hull Corporation but the Bill was supported by the leading businessmen, including Charles Wilson and James Stuart, a prominent seed-crusher, who were undoubtedly influenced by the possibility of future competition from the Manchester Ship Canal, which opened on 1 January 1894.

Between 1893 and 1899, when Alexandra Dock was extended, the value of goods exported from Hull rose slightly but a more substantial rise in import values occurred. Improvements were still needed and in the second half of the 1890s further attempts were made to increase the facilities at the port. In 1895 a proposed amalgamation of the Hull and Barnsley with the North Eastern Company was rejected by a large majority of the Chamber of Commerce, although it was supported by the largest shipowners. Further attempts to reach agreement were made but it was not until 1899 that the Hull Joint Dock Act was passed, despite opposition from Hull Corporation. From that time 'there existed a tacit understanding between the two railway companies'.[76] The fortunes of the Hull and Barnsley improved and dividends were paid in some years on the ordinary stock, whereas up to that time the shareholders had had little return on their investment. So far as additional dock facilities were concerned Hull had to wait until 1914 before the new King George Dock, owned jointly by the North Eastern Railway Co. and the Hull and Barnsley Railway Co., was opened.

*   *   *

The Hull import trade during the last quarter of the century, while resembling earlier decades in composition, reflected changes in the national pattern of trade during the 1870s. These changes included a growth in wheat imports from America, a trade fostered considerably at Hull when, in 1875, Thomas Wilson, Sons & Co. opened a direct shipping line between the port and New York. Some Australian wheat was landed at Hull in the following year and supplies of this grain from California, Chile, Egypt and Oregon also arrived at the port. In 1877, when wheat imports at Hull rose to 953,000 qtrs.—the highest level yet recorded, American wheat accounted for nearly half this total. Between 1880 and 1890 wheat imports doubled; in the latter year two million quarters were landed at the port. Hull's share of the national wheat trade rose from four per cent in the early 1870s to seventeen per cent by 1900. Contributory factors in the growth of this trade were the expansion of flour milling and the new dock facilities. Automatic machinery for flour production was being used in America in the late 1870s and flour imports to Britain doubled between 1878 and 1883. This threat to the home flour market induced local millers to invest in the new plant, first introduced to Hull in 1884, and Joseph Rank, son of James Rank, soon followed. He had commenced business on his own account in 1875 at a windmill in east Hull and about 1883 saw one of the new roller systems. Two years later he opened a mill equipped with Henry Simon roller machinery. Thereafter his business expanded rapidly; another mill was opened in 1891, giving him direct

---

[76] C. D. Parkes, *The Hull and Barnsley Railway* (1946), p.5.

access to wheat cargoes from barges brought alongside the mill, and by 1898 a further building was erected. His mills were then among the largest in the U.K. and in the following year the business was converted to limited liability, with an authorised capital of £700,000.

Some of the smaller millers had closed down, including the Hull Anti-Mill and the Subscription Mill, but other millers had come to Hull, attracted by the availability of imported wheat supplies. Towards the end of the 1870s two country millers had commenced business in Hull: J. G. & L. Thompson, of Skidby, and R. T. Kirby, of Nafferton. In the following decade D. Hurtley & Sons came from Malton and at the end of the century three West Riding firms, which combined to form a new business, Rishworth, Ingleby & Lofthouse, opened mills in Hull on 1 July 1900. Joseph Rank Ltd., however, had emerged as the principal flour-mill establishment; at least half the total flour output from Hull mills, of 1.2 mill. sacks in 1898, being from Rank's mills. In value terms the grain trade at Hull in the 1890s accounted for about a fifth of total imports or about the same as that of the provision trade (see Table V).

Hull had a long tradition of handling groceries, which in the early decades of the century included products mainly from Mediterranean and semi-tropical lands, but in the later 19th century the provision trade was chiefly with Northern Europe and especially Denmark. Hull's location naturally favoured this traffic, which expanded rapidly in the late 1870s; between 1877 and 1887 butter imports, which included butterine and margarine, rose from 40,300 cwts. to 493,000 cwts. Grimsby and to a lesser extent Goole also engaged in this traffic and in the 1890s the Humber ports handled about 30 per cent of the U.K. total. Other provisions included bacon and hams, eggs, lard and meat. Trade in American bacon and hams followed the opening of the direct shipping line with America, but local imports were restricted owing to the superiority of Liverpool for this traffic and after 1890 the quantity imported through Hull declined. Food imports also included citrus and other fruits and vegetables. Fruit merchanting at Hull was extended in response to a growth of fruit imports into Britain in the 1860s. A few firms had been trading in fruit earlier in the century but the first major expansion in this sector occurred in the late 1870s, when the number of merchants rose from sixteen in 1876 to 33 in 1882. Between 1880 and 1899 the quantities of oranges and lemons landed at Hull quadrupled and the port increased its share of the national trade from eight to twelve per cent. By 1900 43 merchants engaged in this trade. Increases also occurred in refined sugar imports, which rose by six times between 1880 and 1890.

The trade in oilseeds, third in value terms at the end of the century, had witnessed changes in the relative importance of the respective seeds. In volume, linseed imports decreased, except for one year—1896—when 1,000,000 qtrs. entered, and the port's share of the U.K. linseed trade declined from about half in 1872 to about a third in the 1890s. Competition from other oil-milling centres in

Britain and abroad was being experienced but, fortunately for the Hull mills, the local paint industry had grown substantially in the second half of the century and provided a market for some of its products. Substitution of cotton seed was, however, another factor in the decline in the Hull linseed trade, for by the late 1870s cotton-seed cakes had to a large extent replaced those made from linseed and rapeseed.[77] Imports of Egyptian cotton seed were supplemented by Indian supplies; linseed, rapeseed and castor seed were also obtained from India at the end of the century. Hull's seed-crushing industry, like flour-milling, participated in the technological developments of the 1870s, when improved crushing machinery was introduced, but until the 1890s the structure of the local industry had not materially changed. Some firms had closed down but were usually replaced by new enterprises and in 1892 the port had about the same number of firms as in the early 1870s. In 1899, however, six of the Hull firms were taken over by the British Oil and Cake Mills Ltd., which brought together mills and oil refineries located mainly in Glasgow, Hull, Liverpool and London. But Hull remained the major British port for oilseed traffic and, in 1900, 50 per cent of the cotton seed, 53 per cent of the rapeseed, 34 per cent of the linseed and almost all the castor seed entering the U.K. from overseas was handled there.

Another of Hull's staple trades, wood, was severely affected by the general economic depression which befell Britain in the late 1870s. In 1879 timber and deal imports were about half those of earlier years in the decade (263,000 tons compared with 510,000 in 1876) and it was about ten years before the level of the mid-1870s was regained. A peak at the end of the 1880s was followed by a minor recession but towards the end of the 1890s, a period of general increases in building activity, imports of hewn and sawn wood exceeded previous levels rising, in 1899, to 820,000 loads. The Hull Chamber of Commerce's *General Price Current* for that year reported conditions of prosperity in the timber trade which had not been experienced for 25 years. It was during these decades that hewn timber imports grew more rapidly than those of sawn wood (deals etc.) and this coincided with a growth in saw-milling at the port. Several new firms specialising in the manufacture of wood products for builders were established and wood was also required for box-making. The port also handled increased imports of pit props and mining timber for the coal industry.

A new commodity, petroleum, was first imported at Hull in the 1870s. This came mainly from America and imports increased rapidly, trebling during the 1880s and rising by more than two and a half times between 1890 and 1900. Raw wool imports, which had declined between 1840 and 1870 became increasingly important in the last decades of the century, rising from 5.4 mill. lbs. in 1870 to 31.5 mill. in 1900. Like wood imports, however, their value in relation to the total trade of the port was low. Flax, one of the principal imports in the earlier decades, became relatively and

---

[77] Hull Chamber of Commerce, *General Price Current* (1879).

absolutely less important in the second half of the century. An allied trade, hemp, also declined in significance due, no doubt, to the declining demand from sail-makers, with the growth of steam shipping, and from rope-makers, with the increased use of wire. In contrast, paper imports trebled between 1890 and 1900 and the volume of hides and iron imports also increased.

Except for 1893, when a dock strike disrupted the port's trade, total import values rose continuously, even though some competition was being experienced from other east coast ports and, after 1894, from the newly opened port of Manchester. The growth of inwards traffic from American and Asian countries reduced the port's earlier dependance on Northern Europe, but even so just over 60 per cent of the tonnage entering from overseas in 1900 was from the latter area. The principal changes were in the U.S.A. trade, from one per cent of inward tonnages in 1870 to thirteen per cent ten years later, a proportion that was more or less maintained to the end of the century (see Table II). Trade with South America also rose (two per cent in 1870, six per cent in 1900), mainly due to imports of linseed and meat. The growth of trade with Africa, especially Egypt, and the import of wheat and oilseeds from India further extended the trading activities of the port. In 1877 and 1884 the import and export trades at Hull were nearly equal in value (imports £18.9 mill., exports £17.8 mill. in 1877, and £18.8 mill. and £19.3 mill. respectively in 1884) but thereafter imports expanded more rapidly and the margin between the two widened considerably. The inclusion of the re-export trade from 1882 in the official trade statistics improved the export position for the years 1885-7 but from then on imports exceeded exports and re-exports together.

Competition from other Humber ports continued to affect the volume of textile exports handled at Hull, and Hull's share of the U.K. trade in these commodities, so high in the early decades of the century, had considerably declined by the end of it (see Table IV). Of the items which accounted for over 80 per cent of Hull's export trade, only two, coal and sheep's and lambs' wool had higher shares of national exports in 1900 than in 1870. From Diagram I it is apparent that Hull did not share in the rapid growth of British exports to Europe which in the 1890s reached the level, in relative terms, of the 1870s. But it was the increased coal traffic which was the outstanding export development in the last quarter of the century, especially after the opening of Alexandra Dock. In 1886 28 per cent of coal exports were shipped from the dock and by 1900 the proportion had risen to 61 per cent. Except for a severe decline owing to the 1893 dock strike, coal shipped to overseas markets exceeded 1,000,000 tons per annum during most of the 1890s, and in 1900 2.2 mill. tons left the port. By value coal exports rose from less than one per cent of all Hull exports in 1870 to ten per cent in 1900. Even so, the Hull coal trade was much below that of the two major coal ports, Cardiff and Newcastle, and accounted for only five per cent of total U.K. coal exports at the turn of the century. In this trade, as in other commodities, Grimsby and Goole continued to compete with Hull. In the 1890s they accounted, in most years, for more than half the Humber coal exports, but in 1900 Hull's share of the total rose to 53 per cent.

Hull's export trade in the later 19th century reflected the growing diversification of the British economy with a wider range of products being shipped from the port. The major changes included the decline in textile traffic, although this was more pronounced at Hull where reduced quantities of linen and woollen goods shipped from the port contrasted somewhat with the trends at Grimsby and Goole, where exports of linen piece goods and woollen and worsted yarn had increased. In mid-century about three-quarters of British yarn exports were sent from Hull but by 1875 Hull's share had declined to 54 per cent and in 1900 was only 26 per cent. From the Humber as a whole, however, 90 per cent of the U.K. exports of these goods were shipped to overseas markets, reflecting the growth of Grimsby and Goole in this traffic. The expansion of the European wool textile industry in the second half of the century, coupled with protective tariff policies, had reduced the demand for many British wool textiles but a market remained for the semi-manufactured products such as tops and noils. Cotton yarns, previously a major Hull export, declined both relatively and absolutely, although exports of these goods through Grimsby and Goole increased in the 1880s and early 1890s. In cotton piece goods, the quantities being shipped from Hull rose in the years from 1875 to 1900 but at a rate equal to national trends since Hull's share, never particularly large, remained at two per cent of the U.K. total throughout the period. Machinery exports from Hull which, by value, equalled cotton yarns and manufactures in 1900 also showed declines relatively to U.K. exports—from nearly a third in 1880 to less than 20 per cent ten years later. Seed oil, a local product, was about 30 per cent of the national export in 1900 compared with 50 per cent in 1870.

By the early 1870s some £23 mill. of British exports passed through Hull but its share of Humber export traffic had declined from over 90 per cent in the late 1850s to 53 per cent in 1872, due primarily to a rapid growth in exports from Grimsby in the late 1860s. Although in 1873-4 Hull's share rose temporarily to nearly 70 per cent, during the subsequent years to 1900 the values of its export traffic declined. In 1900 the Hull exports were only £17 mill., whereas Goole's export traffic had steadily risen from £1.3 mill. in 1874 to £6.9 mill. in 1896. In the late 1890s less than half of the U.K. exports shipped from the Humber ports was handled at Hull. Hull's export pattern differed from national trends in so far as the value of British goods shipped from the port was less in the 1880s and 1890s than in the 1870s, whereas the values of total U.K. exports of British produce and manufactures rose. Hull's share of national exports therefore declined, from ten per cent in the mid-1870s to 5.8 per cent in 1900, although this decline was partly mitigated by an increase in the re-export of imported merchandise. Re-exports from Hull, which included raw cotton, wool, hides, metals and provisions, exceeded the national growth rate for this traffic in the late 1880s and 1890s. Hull's share in this traffic rose from 5.3 per cent of the U.K. total in 1884 to 10.5 per cent in 1898, the peak year for Hull when re-exports, valued at £6.4 mill., were nearly 40 per cent of the home-produced exports (£16.4 mill.) which were shipped from Hull in that year.

The values of the three sectors of trade (imports, exports and re-exports) when added together and expressed as percentages of the total U.K. trade for each year from 1882, when complete data were first available, to 1900 show that Hull's share fluctuated between such narrow limits as 5.9 per cent in 1883 and 6.8 per cent in 1898. Individually, as the earlier analysis has shown, the different sectors exhibited contrasting trends, with exports declining, re-exports varying from five to ten per cent of U.K. totals, and imports rising fairly consistently and at a faster rate than for the country as a whole. In Hull's total trade, imports increased from 46 per cent in 1882 to 58 per cent in 1900 and thus became predominant in the trade pattern of the port. In the latter year also Glasgow replaced Hull as Britain's third port for exports—a position the Humber port had held since comparative records were first available in 1833—but in total trade Hull still maintained its third place, although much below the two leaders, London and Liverpool.[78] In terms of Humber trade, Hull's share had declined slightly from 66 per cent in the 1880s to an average of 63 per cent in the 1890s.

*　　*　　*

Steam shipping at Hull did not maintain the rapid growth rate of the late 1860s and early 1870s and a revival in the popularity of the sailing vessel occurred in the later seventies. A national phenomenon, this was attributed partly to the mid-seventies depression in shipping and shipbuilding which 'favoured sail against steam'. Partly also it was due to the use of the fast clippers which brought grain from America, rice from South-east Asia, wool and grain from Australia and tea from China and could be utilised more economically, at that time, than the steamship.[79]

Between 1873 and 1877 U.K. sailing tonnages rose by four per cent and thereafter declined, but at Hull the increase was continuous for ten years (1873-82) and amounted to a 40 per cent rise in sailing tonnage over this period. The local sailing expansion was due, almost entirely, to the growth of trawl-fishing, which at that time was confined to sailing craft. In 1874 of 740 vessels registered at the port, totalling 175,600 tons, 541, of 38,800 tons, were sailing craft. By 1880 nearly a quarter of the tonnage (46,800 out of 189,400) was propelled by sail and in 1882 sailing tonnages, which rose to 49,000, were on a par with those of 1861. After 1883, however, sailing tonnages declined and by 1900 Hull had only 239 sailing craft, of 15,000 tons, on its register, which represented only six per cent of the 226,600 registered tonnage of the port, consisting of 882 vessels. Relative to U.K. trends, Hull's share of national steamship tonnages had declined to only three per cent by 1900.

---

[78] Total trade at London in 1900 was valued at £267.4 mill., at Liverpool £227.3 mill., but at Hull only £53.6 mill.

[79] Graham, 'Ascendancy of Sailing Ship', pp. 84-5.

Steam capstans were fitted to the trawlers in the 1860s but it was not until the early 1880s that steam was introduced to vessels carrying the fish direct to London from the fishing grounds. Between the late 1850s and early 1880s the average size of the fishing boats rose from 50 to 75 tons, and the addition of steam machinery had enhanced their cost, which in 1882 was more than double that of 20 years earlier.[80] Some 420 smacks sailed from the port in the early 1880s, representing a capital investment of about £500,000. Fishing vessel ownership at that time was more widely spread than the ownership of merchant shipping in the port. In 1878, for example, of the 95 owners with two or more vessels, two (John Holmes and A. W. Ansell) had seventeen and eleven smacks respectively, 44 owners had from three to eight smacks, and 49 had only two smacks each. About 90 others had only one smack.[81] Many of the smacks were locally built after the 1850s and, although steam was introduced in the 1880s, sailing vessels continued to be used for fishing.

In the 1870s two merchant shipping firms transferred their business away from Hull: Dunkerley & Co. passed over its ships to the Newcastle Steam Shipping Co. and C. M. Norwood (M.P. for Hull in 1865-85) removed his vessels to London. A further attempt to form a joint-stock shipping company was made in 1875, with the promotion of the Hull Steam Shipping Co. but like the earlier companies this failed after a few years. The pattern of shipowning during the second half of the century was based primarily on the growth of a few large firms, the most prominent being T. Wilson, Sons & Co., and on a considerable number of smaller ones. For the most part the firms were run on partnership lines with the principals actively engaged in conducting the business.

In 1874 the Wilsons entered the Hull to Newcastle coasting trade, maintaining a regular service. They had also commissioned more steamships from Earle's and other builders, in Hull and elsewhere, for their New York service, inaugurated in 1875. Three years later the Wilsons purchased the fleet of Brownlow, Marsden & Co. (formerly Brownlow, Pearson & Co.), whose ships had engaged in the Hamburg, Antwerp and Dunkirk trades. In that year (1878) the Wilsons owned at least 50,000[82] of Hull's registered tonnage, a quarter of the total, and over a third of Hull's steamship tonnage. By 1880 their fleet had risen to 69,200 tons[83] and in 1881-2 to 77,400,[84] of which 88 per cent was from local shipyards, 76 per cent from Earle's alone.

Bailey & Leetham, the second-largest shipowners in Hull, had 27 ships, of 33,554 tons, in 1880 when over a third of their fleet was locally built. Their ships sailed to Lisbon, St. Petersburg, Königsberg, Copenhagen, other Baltic ports and Hamburg, and also—from

---

[80] *H. & E.C.H.*, 21 Sept. 1882.
[81] Eastern Morning News, *Trade and Commerce of Hull* (1878), pp. 138-46.
[82] List of shipowners as registered on 31 Dec. 1878: M.M.
[83] *M. of P.*, H. of L., Hull and Barnsley Railway and Dock Bill (1880), Q.265.
[84] Obtained from *Liverpool Underwriters' Registry for Iron Vessels* (1881-2) and Registers of Ships' Particulars, Ellerman's Wilson Line Ltd.

London—to Venice, Trieste, Palermo and other Mediterranean ports. Henry Briggs, with fourteen ships, of 21,700 tons, came third. A Hull shipbroker in 1859, he had a capital of £60,000 by 1874 and was joined by his son. Their shipping activities included the carrying of coal from Grimsby to Alexandria, returning to Hull with cotton seed and grain.[85] By contrast with the Wilson and Bailey & Leetham fleets, all Briggs's ships in 1881-2 had been built at Stockton and Sunderland. Nine other firms, owning between four and seven ships each, accounted for 21 per cent of Hull's steamship tonnage and the remaining eighteen per cent was divided between 26 firms with fewer than four ships each. Some of these firms also owned sailing vessels.

In the 1880s and 1890s the Wilson fleet increased, but only 50 per cent of the ships were obtained from Hull yards, a number having been purchased from Tyne and Tees builders in 1885-97. Earle's Shipbuilding Co. went into voluntary liquidation in 1900 but in the following year was purchased by Charles Wilson and thereafter conducted as a private company. In 1903 T. Wilson, Sons & Co., which had a capital of £2 mill. (fully paid), acquired the Bailey & Leetham fleet of 23 vessels and then had a fleet of 105 ships, totalling 170,000 tons. Henry Briggs had closed down a few years earlier and it was not, therefore, surprising that the voice of Charles Wilson was so frequently heard when matters concerning the port's communications were being considered. In addition to his business connections with Hull, he served as an M.P. for the borough from 1874 to 1905, when he became Lord Nunburnholme.

Other voices were also being heard in protest about inadequate facilities; the larger trawler-owners, like the whaling ship owners in the early decades of the century, had become a powerful force in the port's economy by the 1890s. In 1880 the Hull Steam Fishing and Ice Co. Ltd. was formed by some of the smack-owners to purchase screw steamships for use as fish carriers. The shareholders included 43 smack-owners, seven fish merchants and some fish salesmen from London, Leeds, Birmingham and other towns. Five carriers were built for the company by Earle's, which also built a similar vessel in 1882 for the Great Northern Steamship Fishing Co. Ltd., formed in 1880 by members of the Hellyer family and other Hull smack-owners. The first successful steam trawlers were introduced at Grimsby in 1882 and at Hull in 1885. Among the pioneers in the use of steam on fishing craft were the three firms of G. Beeching, Pickering & Haldane, and the Hull Steam Fishing and Ice Co. The establishment of the shipbuilding firm of Cook, Welton & Gemmell in Hull encouraged the use of steam trawlers. Cook and Welton had been platers at Earle's, and Gemmell was a naval architect and designer at the same firm. Their first ship was an iron sailing smack of 92 tons for R. Hellyer, launched in 1885, but by the year's end the partners had built eight sailing trawlers and a steam trawler. At the turn of the century, when the firm transferred to Beverley, about 350 trawlers had been built, almost all being steam-propelled.

[85] Eastern Morning News, *Trade and Commerce of Hull* (1878), p. 119.

Several new trawling companies were established in the 1880s: these included the Humber Steam Trawling Co. Ltd., with a paid-up capital of about £40,000 in 1891, and the British Steam Trawling Co. Ltd., with a paid-up capital of £27,200. About the same time some of the principal trawler-owners were converting their own firms to limited liability: these included Pickering & Haldane in 1889 and C. Hellyer in 1891. In 1890 the Hull fish merchants, of whom there were nearly 100 in 1892, established their own protection association and in the latter year the Hull Fishing Vessel Owners' Association Ltd. brought together the trawler-owners.

By the early 1890s the trawler-owners were agitating for improved dock accommodation, meetings being held with the Hull Dock Company and the North Eastern Railway Company in 1891 and 1893. One of the principal owners, C. Hellyer, stated in 1891 [86] that their trade was believed to be a valuable source of revenue to the dock company and the railway company but that it was apparently considered of little value. In 1894, the year following the take-over of the dock company by the railway company, Mr. Hellyer remarked that the railway 'held the destiny of the fishing trade in their hands'.[87] The trawler-owners threatened to leave Hull, requesting accommodation at Grimsby and Boston, but at that time Grimsby was unable to take further vessels. A fortnight later, however, the Midland Railway, which served Grimsby, agreed to spend £250,000 on facilities there. This action induced the North Eastern Railway to sanction additional facilities at Hull for the fishing trade; an extension to St. Andrew's Dock was opened in 1897 which almost doubled the area available to the fishing industry. Charles Wilson's influence also extended to this sector of the port's economy for in 1890, when the Hull Steam Fishing and Ice Co. Ltd. was reconstructed with an authorised capital of £200,000, of which some £63,200 was paid-up, he was chairman of the company.

Coastwise shipping, which declined relatively to overseas shipping in the 1840s and 1850s, expanded in the second half of the century due to increases in shipments of coal: between 1880 and 1890, for example, coastwise coal shipments rose from 26,700 tons to 328,500 tons. Other goods carried coastwise included oilcake, grain and timber. Steamships were used in the coastal trade in the 1840s but during most of the 1850s and 1860s the tonnages clearing the port in sailing craft exceeded those in steamships. Between 1870 and the first decade of the 20th century, however, tonnages of sailing vessels cleared coastwise declined from nearly half of the total coastwise traffic to about ten per cent. This traffic, with an emphasis on outward shipments (mainly comprising goods previously imported at Hull, local products and coal) differed from that of overseas trade, in which shipping entering Hull (with cargoes or in ballast) exceeded the tonnages cleared from the port. This trend was especially marked from the 1840s to the 1860s, when inter-port competition was increasing but the discrepancies between tonnages of entrances

---

[86] *H.N.* 28 Nov. 1891.
[87] *H.N.* 9 June 1894.

and clearances of ships at Hull were somewhat reduced with the increased coal exports of the later decades. Among the firms engaging in river and canal traffic was that of Furley & Co., which originated in Gainsborough but had opened a Hull office by the early 1830s. The firm participated for a time in coastwise traffic between Hull and Newcastle, other east coast ports, and London but in later years was concerned with river and canal traffic between Sheffield and the Humber, which included iron ore for the steel works and return cargoes of rails, axles, springs and the like. It also carried china clay, black lead and ground gannister—a Midland grit highly prized in the manufacture of silica bricks.

There is little doubt that had Alexandra Dock not been provided by the independent company, or a dock of similar size by the Hull Dock Company itself, the port's trading activities would have suffered more than they did. From the 1870s to 1900 shipping tonnages frequenting the Hull docks more than doubled, from 2 mill. to 4.2 mill., accounting for 5.4 per cent of total inwards tonnages at U.K. ports. The growth in port traffic was reflected in the increase of workers in transport activities—including those on the railways, roads, seas, rivers, docks and harbours—from 10,490 in 1881 to 21,560 in 1901. Nearly 30 per cent of total occupied males and over a fifth of the working population of Hull were employed in these trades in 1901. At the end of the century, therefore, a large proportion of Hull's 240,259 inhabitants was dependent directly or indirectly on its trading activities.

The fishing industry had also become of major importance in the port's economy. The capital invested in the steam trawlers was estimated in 1900 at £1,360,000 and in three large ice houses at £125,000. With 30 houses for smoking fish, premises for repairing and fitting out ships, and the dock and railway facilities, the industry's total capital amounted to several million pounds.[88] It was also estimated that at least 10,000 persons were directly employed by the industry, of whom 3,500 were trawlermen, about 2,000 in the ship-building and engineering yards specialising on work for the fishing industry, the same number in fitting out the ships, about 1,000 in the smoke houses, 500 on the fish market and the remainder working in ice manufacture, rope and twine spinning and the making of nets. The Hull fishing industry had become, in the last quarter of the 19th century, a dominant sector of the trade and shipping of the port.

---

[88] *H.N.* 3 Feb. 1900.

V

The Mercantile Community

Nearly half of the 300 or so members of the mercantile community in the early years of the century were general merchants dealing in a variety of commodities. Of the remainder, the most numerous of the specialist merchants were those trading in wood and in wines and spirits. Commission agents and brokers were also essential to the trading sector and, in response to the growth of overseas trade at the port in the 1820s and 1830s, their numbers increased. In 1838, for example, at least 86 were specifically listed as general agents in White's *Directory of the West Riding and Hull and York*. At this time also nearly 70 firms combined merchanting with shipowning, ship and insurance broking, or acting as commission agents, in addition to 48 who were merchants alone. Other categories, which included ship and insurance brokers, sloop brokers and wharfingers, had nearly 20 firms. The mercantile pattern was complicated by the fact that most of the 35 shipowners or sloop-owners noted by White were already included in one or other of the previous groups. In all, however, approximately 220 firms were known to be engaged in some form of general merchanting, agency or broking work. The specialised merchants are easier to detect. Their numbers had also risen and included 48 dealing in wines and/or spirits, 27 in corn, 30 in timber and 26 in coal. In addition, six merchants dealt in bark and hide, six in iron, four each in paper and lead, and two in hemp. There were also nine banks in the town. Taken together, therefore, the general and specialised merchants and agents numbered about 380 or so in the late 1830s.

By mid-century firms engaged in mercantile activities had risen to over 400; the earlier expansion among the commission agents had continued and of the principal specialist groups those dealing in corn had increased the most—from 27 to 39 between 1838 and 1851. About the same number of firms were trading in wood and wines as in the 1830s but the wholesale fruit merchants had risen from two to five and those dealing in coal had doubled, to 53. The mercantile community of the 1850s included long-established, reputable and quite often wealthy business houses. The iron merchants J. Sykes & Sons, for example, had a capital of £90,000 in 1853, the timber merchants Barkworth & Spaldin had £40,000-50,000 capital in 1847, and R. & J. Harrison, also in timber, had £130,000 exclusive of the value of ships they owned in 1851. John Beadle & Co., stated by the Bank of England agent to be one of the most wealthy firms in Hull in the early 1830s, had a capital of £50,000 and annual returns of at least £120,000 in 1850.

The mercantile community included some long-established firms engaged in the corn trade, notoriously speculative in character. Some of these firms, of long standing and locally well known, were considered credit-worthy by Hull bankers, but in fact were obtaining financial assistance for other speculative enterprises. Among these were H. S. Bright, of Taylor & Bright, and S. T. Hassell, originally of Halls, Todd & Hassell, a firm founded in the 18th century. Both men were heavily committed to the Hull cotton industry and, in addition, had other financial interests. Hassell engaged in the flotation of various unsuccessful companies, which he financed largely through credit from Harrison, Watson & Co., Hull bankers. When the bank was compelled to suspend payments at the time of severe credit contraction in 1857 the debts against Hassell amounted to £140,407, for which the bank held securities valued at only £10,510. Between 1856 and 1857 Bright was allowed to increase his overdraft with the same bank from £22,300 to £93,000, as he was believed to be 'a man of property', but when the bank closed he had debts of £101,438, of which £86,107 was owed to the bank. It was largely through the activities of these men that the bank failed in 1857. By contrast, other principal merchant firms in mid-century were J. T. & N. Hill, which had been in business since the 1830s and by 1862 had a capital of £50,000; Veltmann & Co., shipping and forwarding agents, with a capital of £34,000 in 1868; and Beadle, Sykes & Co., with a capital of £60,000 in 1872. At the lower end of the mercantile structure were many small firms with limited resources which operated on a restricted scale and were frequently of short duration.

In the second half of the century the widening of the port's trading activities was reflected in the size of the mercantile sector. At the major growth points there were increased numbers of coal merchants, exporters and dealers, provision merchants, members of the corn and seed trades, oil merchants, and fish and fruit merchants. Overlapping of functions again complicated the mercantile pattern but by the early 1890s at least 1,200 firms or individuals, excluding employees, were directly associated with some form of mercantile activity. Among the largest groups were those trading in coal, of whom there were 85 merchants (fourteen of whom were exporters) and 144 dealers. Corn and seed merchants totalled about 100, fish merchants nearly 100, forwarding and shipping agents over 70, some of whom were also shipowners, and there were nearly 50 ship and insurance brokers. Some expansion had occurred in the timber trade but of the 52 firms dealing in wood, only thirteen were importers. Numbers in the wine and spirit trade remained fairly static throughout the century and totalled 44 in 1892, but the firms specialising in provisions had increased with the expansion of trade in these goods; produce merchants, provision merchants and wholesale grocers totalled about 50 in that year. The general merchant class, so prominent in the earlier decades of the century, numbered fewer than 40 and had obviously been affected by the growing specialisation of the mercantile functions.

Some of the Hull merchants participated actively in the provision of regular steamship services to continental ports. They included Brown, Atkinson & Co., Gee & Co., W. & C. L. Ringrose, and T. Wilson, Sons & Co. Towards the end of the fifties a comparative newcomer to the shipowning business, Z. C. Pearson, originally a master mariner, became heavily involved in the mortgaging of ships. He took part in an attempt to break the blockade of the ports of the southern states of America during the civil war and became bankrupt in the early 1860s with debts of £648,000. However, only a few of the master mariners, of whom nearly 230 lived in Hull in the early 1850s, were also recorded as shipowners.

Changes in the shipowning pattern of the port, mentioned earlier, had concentrated a large part of the local shipping in the hands of T. Wilson, Sons & Co. The company was also associated with other activities, especially shipbuilding, marine engineering[89] and trawling, a combination of activities which resembled the pattern of the early 19th century when shipowning was often combined with either manufacturing or some form of mercantile interests. In 1892 Hull had about 40 firms of shipowners, excluding trawler-, smack- and sloop-owners, of whom there were more than 60. In addition fourteen steam navigation companies with vessels trading at the port had local representatives acting as agents or managers.

When the Hull Chamber of Commerce was established on 1 March 1837 its 108 founder-members, although representing less than a third of the mercantile community, reflected to a considerable extent the main groups associated with the commercial activities of the port. The most numerous were the general agents (27), general merchants (19), shipowners (12) and insurance brokers (10). The timber merchants, among the largest of the specialised groups, were poorly represented, with only three of their number among the founder-members. Only five of the large number of wine and spirit merchants had joined but two out of the six hide and bark merchants and five of the corn merchants were members. Three of the principal bankers—George Liddell, James Henwood and Robert Raikes, jun.—had also joined. The industrial sector, still relatively small in the port's economy, was represented by two paint-makers, Henry Blundell and William Tudor (who specialised in white lead), a sack-maker, William Jameson, a soap-maker, William Jackson, a glue-maker, Robert Wake, and the shipbuilder, Edward Gibson.

Among the early interests of the Chamber of Commerce were the establishment of telegraphic communication, discussions on decimal coinage, the repealing of customs duties and changes in the navigation laws, in addition to its concern with improvements in local port facilities. The chamber also took an active part in attempts to abolish the Stade and Sound dues. The former were levied by Hanover on goods passing through the Elbe and were collected at Hamburg. The latter were levied by Denmark on all merchant vessels entering the Baltic. A toll was also levied on shipping using the River Scheldt, in Belgium, and from 1837 to the early 1860s, when the last of these dues was abolished, the Hull chamber pressed for governmental action.

The Shipowners' Society amalgamated with the Chamber of Commerce in 1847 and the latter added 'Shipping' to its title. In the early 1850s the chamber took an active part in the campaign for the

---

[89] Arthur Wilson was a 'sleeping partner' in Amos & Smith, marine engineers.

reduction of dock dues but during the fifties, when for five consecutive years S. T. Hassell was chairman, the chamber did not receive the support from the mercantile community which had been expected, and membership declined. In 1855 Henry Blundell emphasised the dependence of Hull's trade and commerce on the shipping interest and in the late 1850s and early 1860s the presidents of the chamber included some of the more prominent shipowners of the port, H. J. Atkinson, J. Lumsden, C. M. Norwood and J. R. Ringrose. It was asserted in the 1880s that the chamber's interest in shipping had discouraged the expansion of membership but this was remedied with the expansion of the industrial sector in the later years of the century.

Until the establishment of trade associations by some of the major mercantile groups[90] towards the end of the century, the Chamber of Commerce and the Hull Guardian Society[91] were the main local organisations serving the interests of the mercantile sector of the port. Nevertheless, a complaint frequently heard during the second half of the century related to the chamber's inability to increase its membership proportionately to the growth of the mercantile firms. Many of the largest mercantile businesses were members but some were not. A few of the principal trawler-owners had joined the chamber but in general the fishing industry was somewhat detached from the other commercial sectors of the port, and even some of the latter were not well represented. Furthermore, few members of Hull Corporation came from the mercantile community and few members of the chamber were shareholders of the Hull Dock Company. The extent to which some or all of these factors contributed to the dissensions which beset the town on the matter of improved port communications cannot be assessed but it seems a reasonable assumption that they aggravated the conflict between the various sectors.

*   *   *

There was a high mortality rate of mercantile firms in Hull. Few of the many firms in business throughout these decades survived over long periods. The rate of entry and exit was particularly high in the timber, corn and fruit trades. Rather more stability was apparent in the iron, wine and spirit and coal trades. The trades which showed little growth in numbers were those dealing with hemp, flax, skin, leather and iron. During the second half of the century the overall number of firms increased about threefold but many of these were small. Towards the end of the century, however, new firms, attracted by the possibilities for extending the trade of the port, were established and in the first decade of the 20th century were stated to be supplying the flour mills and seed-

---

[90] The corn trade had its own association at the end of the 1880s, the seed, oil and cake trade had also formed an association which was affiliated to the Hull chamber in 1892, and by the end of the century the fruit buyers and coal exporters had their own organisations.

[91] Founded in 1827 to protect the interests of the local shopkeepers.

crushing and oil-extracting mills with seven-tenths of their raw materials.[92]

The Bank of England branch at Hull, with lending policies dictated from London that were more conservative than those of the private banks, had comparatively few customers. At mid-century the small amount of 'first-class' paper negotiated at Hull went to the other bankers. The Bank of England required customers to commit themselves to a fixed deposit and maintain a certain balance; but as few of the firms were, in 1846, 'on the right side with their own bankers' they could not 'afford to leave an unremunerative balance on their account at the Branch' since no interest was paid on deposit accounts at branches of the Bank. The agent admitted, however, in 1851 when the banker George Liddell died, that Pease & Liddell had 'the lion's share of the business of this place' and that there was no one to take Liddell's place. Smith Bros. & Co., who with Pease & Liddell handled the accounts of many of the principal firms in Hull, had, in the earlier decades, adopted a less liberal policy than Pease & Liddell but by the early 1860s were engaging on a considerable scale in the financing of mercantile activities. One of the partners of Smith, Payne & Smith, its parent bank in London, in a letter in 1861 to a colleague, who was a partner in both the London and Hull banks, commented:

> you are quite aware of the strong opinion which I entertain as to the system pursued at the Hull bank, in making very large advances to various mercantile, & other Firms, in the Town for long, & uncertain periods, & leaning upon the Banking House *in London*, for such advances! This custom is radically opposed to all sound principles, pregnant with difficulty, anxiety & danger especially in such critical times as the present. *It must not be continued* . . .[93]

Whether any amendments were made to the policies of Smith Bros. at that time is not known but in the following decade, when a corn merchant, Castle Kelsey, failed with liabilities of about £80,000, among his unsecured creditors were Smith Bros., to whom he owed £23,000.

The policies of the Hull Banking Co., the first Hull joint-stock bank (established in 1833), were both generous and rigid on occasions. During its 60-year history (it was merged with the York City and County Bank in 1894) many overdrafts of several thousand pounds each were permitted without security, although there is some evidence that large overdrafts were usually about ten per cent of expected turnover—a ratio also used by Smith Bros. & Co. Generous overdrafts were sometimes allowed when the whole of a particular firm's business was transacted at the bank, for, in the 19th century, it was customary for firms to deal with two or more bankers at a time. However, the Hull Banking Co. often requested some form of security, which frequently included assets not immediately

---

[92] These firms were: Ross T. Smyth & Co., R. Proctor, Sons & Co., S. Sanday & Co., Louis Dreyfus, and Ralli Bros.: A.G.M. Hull Chamber of Commerce, 22 Nov. 1905.

[93] Leighton-Boyce, *Smiths the Bankers*, pp. 283-4.

negotiable. Property deeds were accepted, as were bills of sale on ships, stocks of goods such as linseed or timber in local warehouses, personal promissory notes and usually railway shares, although the latter were sometimes refused.

It was not surprising, therefore, that the Hull agent of the Bank of England experienced difficulties in obtaining accounts. He informed the Bank governors in 1849 that the business houses engaged in the iron and wood trades could be the best customers of the branch if longer credit facilities were allowed. In these trades the greater part of the bills were drawn for four to six months, periods in excess of the limit of three months generally permitted by the Bank. It was agreed that the agent should be allowed 'discretionary power to make occasional advances for a month on bills having four months to run to such customers as keep substantial and satisfactory accounts'. The privilege was, however, to be 'exercised with prudence and not used to lead to an extension of the ordinary term of credit'. When he was encouraged to pursuade his customers to keep larger balances he informed the Bank in 1862 that

> it may suit the large capitalists of Liverpool, Manchester and Leeds to have large balances unemployed in the hands of the Bank but my customers are comparatively, if not positively, small men who are in the habit of requiring and receiving uncovered advances from their banker; how can it possibly suit them therefore to leave a remunerative balance in my hands? —one customer carrying on a large and I believe profitable business with a small capital, assured me that he could at any time obtain from his banker an open advance of £10,000.

The contemporary evidence suggests, therefore, that while some of Hull's successful mercantile firms were wealthy, especially in the iron, wood and shipping trades, the majority of firms were heavily dependent upon bank finance. This having been said, it is apparent that the merchants of Hull, with some notable exceptions, of whom the Sykes and Wilson families are outstanding examples, were not equal in wealth or political influence to the leading merchants, shipowners and bankers in other parts of the country. There was no large group in Hull to compare with the great mercantile and shipping families of London, Liverpool or Manchester. Their scale of living, with some exceptions, was rarely on the same affluent level and their political influence in the affairs of Hull was never as dominant as elsewhere.

Conclusion

The widening of Hull's trading connections and the provision of additional dock and rail facilities in the later decades of the century contributed to the expansion in the shipping tonnage frequenting the port, although this, taken alone, is not indicative of the full volume of goods handled. It represents the tonnage of the ships and not the cargoes, but it does provide a useful guide to general trading activity. To some considerable extent the demand from Hull's own expanding oil, paint, flour and saw-milling industries, the growth of which had originally been due largely to the availability of imported raw materials, had contributed to increases in the oilseed, grain and timber trades. The port's location also favoured the growth of the provision trade with Denmark, although competition from the other Humber ports was especially apparent here. In comparison with national trends, however, there is some evidence that the growth of Hull's trade, taken as a whole, and also the tonnage of shipping registered at the port had, in some degree, been retarded. This was particularly seen in Hull's declining share of British exports. The extent to which the responsibility for this can be attached to inadequate communications, competition from other Humber and east coast ports, or lack of local enterprise defies quantitative analysis. Although the investment of much local capital in whaling in the early decades of the century served the community well at the time, it seems likely that the expansion of trade connections with other parts of the world was thereby held back. Contemporary evidence supports this view but it is also likely that local conflicts were detrimental to the port's development at various periods during the century.

The history of dock and railway developments in 19th-century Hull was punctuated by constant battles between the mercantile community, usually but not always supported by the town authorities and the ratepayers generally, and the Hull Dock Company and the North Eastern Railway. There was an almost continuous conflict between the Dock Company and the railway companies using the port from the 1840s to the 1890s. Throughout these decades, repeated references were made to the general failure of the various groups involved to reach common agreement in the interests of the improved working of the port[94] and while facilities were extended they were not wholly satisfactory until the eve of the First World War.

It is difficult to estimate the extent to which inadequate facilities did retard the development of the port. Given the location of Hull on the eastern seaboard, some distance from the main industrial districts which were the obvious catchment areas, it is

---

[94] These included the comments of various local men at meetings of the Hull Chamber of Commerce: H. S. Bright, merchant (19 May 1848); C. M. Norwood, Hull M.P. (A.G.M. 30 Oct. 1879) and Sir A. K. Rollit, Hull lawyer (4 Nov. 1887).

quite probable that an earlier construction of rail links with the interior would have assisted the growth of its trade. The port did reflect to some considerable extent the pattern of British trade with North European countries, and this was especially true in earlier decades, but it hardly participated in the growth of British exports to these areas in the 1890s although, as has been shown, it was handling a quite considerable re-export trade, most of it destined for European countries. How far the overall decline in Hull's share of the British export trade was due to its communication problems cannot be statistically ascertained but there seems little doubt that competition from other east coast ports—especially those on the Humber estuary—and, at the end of the century, from Manchester played an important role. While some of Hull's growing firms, such as Reckitt & Sons Ltd., makers of washing blue, starch, black lead etc., Rose, Downs & Thompson Ltd. (of the Old Foundry), suppliers of oilseed-crushing machinery, and the oilseed and paint manufacturers were supplying overseas markets, Hull was largely dependent for its exports on inland districts. This situation was described by Charles Wilson to the Hull Chamber of Commerce in November 1881, when he said that 'everyone knows that there is very little local export trade at Hull, but at Newcastle there are considerable exports of chemicals and they are also drawing to that port every trans-shipped article that has hitherto been brought to Hull'. It cannot be assumed, however, that the port's import trade would have expanded further had improved facilities been available earlier to supply more return freights in the form of exports of coal and other commodities. The comparative data do reveal, however, that the increased imports countered the decline in exports and enabled Hull to maintain a six per cent share of total British trade during the last decades of the century. Hull's communication problems have, nevertheless, persisted and continue to influence the economic growth of the port in the 20th century.

TABLE I

Hull: Tonnages of Shipping, 1800-1900

Selected years and averages	(A) Tonnages of vessels on which dock dues were paid*		(B) Tonnages of vessels entering from overseas only (including whale-fishing).		(B) as percentage of (A)	(B) as percentage of U.K.
	Thous. tons	Indices (1800=100)	Thous. tons	Indices (1800=100)		
1800	198	100	125	100	63	5.8
1808	82	41	38	30	46	†
1810-14 (av.)	196	99	88	70	45	†
1815	265	134	125	100	47	5.9
1818	342	173	225	180	66	8.5
1815-19 (av.)	281	142	148	118	53	7.1
1820-24 (av.)	308	156	158	126	51	7.6
1825	449	227	328	262	73	10.6
1825-29 (av.)	393	198	247	198	63	9.4
1830	360	182	215	172	60	7.3
1830-34 (av.)	370	187	219	175	59	7.2
1835-39 (av.)	550	278	313	250	57	8.2
1839	703	355	383	306	54	8.6
1840	652	329	349	279	53	7.5
1840-49 (av.)	725	366	384	307	53	6.8
1853	888	448	555	444	62	5.5
1855	782	395	415	332	53	4.6
1856	1,077	544	666	533	62	6.4
1850-59 (av.)	942	476	553	442	59	5.9
1860-69 (av.)	1,233	623	842	674	68	5.8
1872	1,875	947	1,330	1,064	71	6.3
1870-79 (av.)	2,032	1,026	1,361	1,089	67	5.9
1880-89 (av.)	2,568	1,297	1,705	1,364	66	5.4
1890-99 (av.)	3,422	1,728	2,205	1,764	64	5.4
1900	4,215	2,129	2,667	2,134	63	5.4

* These totals include ships frequenting the port upon which dock dues were levied by the Hull Dock Company; from 1893 they relate to the tonnages entering the North Eastern Railway Docks (taken over from the Hull Dock Co.) and the Alexandra Dock (of the Hull and Barnsley Railway Co.), the data for which were included from the opening of this dock in 1885.

† Not available.

Sources:

(A) Huffam MSS.

(B) Hull data: 1800: *M. of E.* Hull Dock Bill (1844); 1808-1832: *A. & P.* 1833 XXXIII; 1833: Gawtress, *Corporation of Hull*, p. 376; 1834-50: *A. & P.* 1851 LII; 1851-2: *Tables of Revenue, Population and Commerce;* 1853-1900: *Trade and Navigation Accounts of the United Kingdom.* U.K. data: 1800: H. of L. MSS. 1 Mar. 1806; 1801-48: *A. & P.* 1849 LII (no data for 1811-13); 1849-52: *Tables of Revenue, Population and Commerce;* 1853-1900 as for Hull above.

TABLE II

Countries of Origin of British and Foreign Shipping Entering Hull, 1808-1900

Percentage of total tonnage entering (excluding whale fisheries)

	1808	1810	1815	1825	1830	1835	1840	1850	1860	1870	1880	1890	1900
Russia	12	18	38	32	32	26	20	21	21	21	18	17	19
Germany	....	5	10	15	19	18	19	22	13	10	18	12	10
Prussia	8	25	12	17	9	9	13	7	12	8	inc. in Germany		
Denmark	—	14	1	9	8	7	9	7	5	3	2	1	1
Sweden	48	23	15	2	3	5	5	6	11	12	9	13	12
Netherlands †	9	1	8	9	13	10	10	14	12	12	10	8	10
Belgium	inc. in Netherlands total					2	1	6	5	5	3	4	3
Norway	with Denmark		4	4	2	2	2	1	3	8	7	9	8
Northern Europe total	77	86	88	88	86	79	79	84	82	79	67	65	63
Other European:													
France	1	....	....	1	1	2	1	1	6	5	4	3	4
Portugal	3	2	2	....	1	1	1	1	1	2	2	1	....
Italy	—	—	1	1	1	1	1	1	1	2	1	2	....
Spain	3	....	1	....	1	....	1	....	....	....	1	1	2
Others	6	2	1	—	—	1	....	....	1	1	—	3	3
U.S.A.	1	3	....	....	....	....	1	2	1	1	13	12	13
B.N.C.*	6	6	4	9	9	16	14	9	5	2	2	....	1
S. America	—	—	—	—	—	—	—	....	....	2	1	1	6
Africa	—	—	—	—	....	....	....	—	1	4	6	6	5
Australia	—	—	—	—	—	—	—	—	—	—	1	....	1
India (inc. East Indies)	—	—	—	—	—	—	—	1	1	—	1	4	1
Others (inc. British. West Indies)	3	1	2	....	....	....	....	—	—	1	....	1	1
	100	100	99+	99+	99+	100	99+	99+	99+	100	99+	99+	99+

* British Northern Colonies (Canada, New Brunswick, Nova Scotia and Prince Edward Island), which became the Dominion of Canada in 1867.

.... Less than 0.6 per cent.

+ Components do not total 100 on account of rounding.

† Flanders and Holland, 1808-1816; Belgium, Flanders and Holland, 1817-32.

Sources: 1808-1830: *A. & P.* 1833 XXXIII; 1835 and 1840: *Tables of Revenue, Population and Commerce;* 1860-1905: *Annual Statements of Navigation and Shipping.*

TABLE III

Estimated Value of Hull Whale Fishery, 1814-33

	No. of ships returning to Hull	Tuns of oil	Price of oil £	Price of oil s.	Value £	Tons of bone (to nearest ton)	Price of bone £	Value £	Total value of oil and bone £
1814	58	7,326	30	0	219,780	291	65	18,915	238,695
1815	56	3,746	41	0	153,586	189	65	12,285	165,871
1816	55	5,155	28	0	144,340	264	60	15,840	160,180
1817	55	4,711	42	0	197,862	245	80	19,600	217,462
1818	63	6,199	40	0	247,960	305	80	24,400	272,360
1819	62	5,183	32	15	169,743	254	70	17,780	187,523
1820	57	8,086	28	0	226,408	403	60	24,180	250,588
1821	53	5,888	20	0	117,760	322	90	28,980	146,740
1822	39	3,112	19	0	59,128	154	180	27,720	86,848
1823	41	5,490	18	0	98,820	297	190	56,430	155,250
1824	36	3,500	19	15	69,125	197	185	36,445	105,570
1825	34	2,873	26	0	74,698	132	300	39,600	114,298
1826	30	2,674	25	0	66,850	148	230	34,040	100,890
1827	29	4,579	18	0	82,422	262	190	49,780	132,202
1828	29	5,297	19	10	103,291	307	200	61,400	164,691
1829	31	3,976	24	0	95,424	220	190	41,800	137,224
1830	20	1,271	45	0	57,195	70	350	24,500	81,695
1831	32	1,797	26	0	46,722	103	180	18,540	65,262
1832	28	4,503	19	0	85,557	253	115	29,095	114,652
1833	26	5,024	18	0	90,432	285	130	37,050	127,482

Source: Gawtress, *Corporation of Hull*, p.382.

Note: H. Munroe, 'Statistics of the Northern Whale Fisheries', *Journal of the Royal Statistical Society*, vol. xvii (1854), pp. 41-2, also provided estimates of the value of the oil and bone obtained for each year from 1772 to 1852, but used average values for oil of £30 per tun and of bone at £200 per ton. The data in the above table show that the use of these averages will not give an accurate result for individual years and, in fact, there are considerable differences between Munroe's figures and those shown above. See also J. T. Jenkins, *A History of the Whale Fisheries* (1921), Appendix VI, where it is stated that 'the annual averages of values of oil and bone are based on estimates made by Munroe and are of doubtful reliability'. The data relating to tuns of oil were in most cases identical with those given in a MS. notebook of whaling statistics, 1772-1842, in the Hull City Library. For a few years, however, there were slight differences between them.

TABLE IV

Export Trade at Hull: Principal Commodities, 1850-1900

(A) *Percentages of total Hull exports of British manufacture (by value)*

	1850	1857	1870	1880	1890	1900
Coal	0·3	0·4	0·7	1·6	3·4	10·1
Cotton goods	15·7	11·9	9·2	10·3	13·2	11·4
Cotton yarns	38·2	31·8	20·9	18·6	17·4	9·1
Hardware	2·6	3·2	4·6	2·0	1·4	1·3
Linen goods	2·6	1·9	2·6	2·3	0·9	0·7
Linen yarns	3·3	4·5	2·9	0·9	0·5	0·6
Machinery	2·4	5·9	8·7	15·4	16·1	20·7
Metals	3·7	7·5	13·8	9·3	7·2	7·2
Seed-oil	†	1·8	3·7	3·4	2·2	2·7
Wool: sheep's & lambs'	—	0·9	0·6	1·4	0·7	6·2
Woollen & worsted goods	13·8	10·5	10·6	7·1	6·8	4·3
Woollen & worsted yarns	12·5	12·6	13·0	10·0	8·1	7·3
Unspecified	3·7	1·7	5·7	10·9	10·3	9·1
	98·8	94·6	97·0	93·2	88·2*	90·7*

* Specified items, in addition to those shown in the table, included a number of miscellaneous commodities, such as chemicals, leather, manures, etc., none of which had an important share of the trade.

† Not available.

Sources:
1850: *A. & P.* 1852-3 XCIX.
1857-1900: *Annual Statements of Trade of the U.K.*

(B) *Percentages of total U.K. exports‡ (by value)*

	1850	1857	1870	1880	1890	1900
Coal	2	2	2	3	3	5
Cotton goods	8	6	3	3	4	3
Cotton yarns	59	58	25	29	25	20
Hardware	12	12	18	10	9	10
Linen goods	3	7	5	5	3	2
Linen yarn	47	43	21	14	10	10
Machinery	36	24	29	31	17	18
Metals	6	6	9	5	3	3
Seed-oil	†	43	50	38	26	29
Wool: sheep's & lambs'	†	13	17	23	15	32
Woollen & worsted goods	20	15	9	8	6	5
Woollen & worsted yarns	94	68	44	56	35	20
Total exports from Hull as percentage of U.K.	14	13	9	8	7	6
Exports from Humber ports as percentage of U.K.	†	14	15	13	12	12

‡ Exports of British manufacture only.

† Not available.

Sources: As in (A).

TABLE V

Import Trade at Hull: Principal Commodities in 1857, 1895 and 1900

Percentages of total imports (by value)

	1857* (estimate)	1895	1900
Cotton (raw)	0·8	3·4	2·1
Flax and hemp	12·0	0·9	0·5
Fruit total	0·8	1·3	1·2
Grains: total	19·9	22·5	20·5
of which *Wheat*	*10·0*	*16·3*	*12·8*
Hides	1·0	1·5	0·8
Metals (inc. iron ore)	7·9	5·0	5·5
Petroleum	—	†	1·0
Provisions: total	1·3	22·2	22·7
of which *Butter*	*0·7*	*10·5*	*9·8*
Bacon and Hams	—	*2·6*	*3·8*
Seeds: total	20·2	5·3	10·2
of which *Linseed*	*18·1*	*4·8*	*4·6*
Cotton seed	—	*3·7*	*4·3*
Rapeseed	*2·1*	†	*0·4*
Sugar: refined	0·2	4·3	2·6
Wood	6·4	4·5	6·6
Wool: sheep's and lambs'	10·8	4·1	4·0
Woollen goods	5·6	2·5	1·3
	86·9	80·7	79·0
Total value of all imports as percentage of U.K.	4·2	6·0	5·9

* Although quantity data on imports at individual ports were published from 1857 and the total value of imports from 1872, it was not until 1895 that detailed value analyses of imports were made available. The figures shown here for 1857 were calculated by taking the average values of the commodities imported into the U.K. and applying these to the Hull quantity data for 1857.

† Not available.

Source: Annual Statements of Trade of the U.K.

DIAGRAM I

DECLARED VALUES OF EXPORTS FROM HULL AND THE HUMBER PORTS AS PERCENTAGES OF TOTAL U.K. EXPORTS, COMPARED WITH THE DECLARED VALUES OF U.K. EXPORTS TO EIGHT NORTH EUROPEAN COUNTRIES AS A PERCENTAGE OF U.K. TOTAL EXPORTS, 1833-1900 (incomplete series)

Key:

——— U.K. exports to Northern Europe

.... Humber ports

——— Hull

The U.K. percentages relate to exports to Belgium, Denmark, Germany, Holland, Norway, Prussia, Russia and Sweden.

Sources:

U.K.	1833-1846	*A. & P.* 1849 LII.
	1847-1852	*Tables of Revenue, Population and Commerce.*
	1853-1900	*Annual Statements of Trade.*
Hull	1833-1850	*A. & P.* 1851 LII.
	1851-1856	*A. & P.* 1854 LX; 1854-5 XLVI; 1856 LV; Sess. 2 1857 XXXIX.
	1857-1900	*Annual Statements of Trade.*
Humber	1852-1854	Huffam MSS. for Grimsby and Goole.
	1857-1900	*Annual Statements of Trade.*

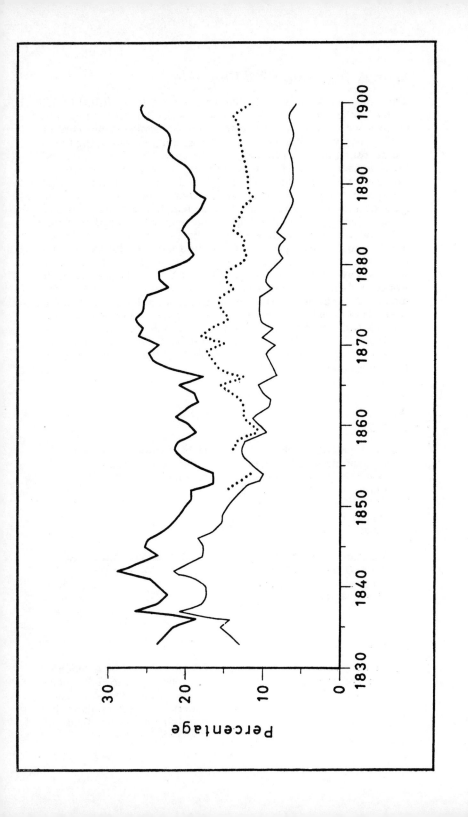

Sources and Select Bibliography

This study has been compiled largely from my unpublished Ph.D. thesis 'Some aspects of the economy of Hull in the nineteenth century with special reference to business history' (University of Hull, 1965), which has a detailed bibliography. Copies of the thesis are deposited in the Brynmor Jones Library, Hull University, and the Kingston upon Hull City Library. In preparing the thesis extensive use was made of official and business records, local newspapers and directories and, where appropriate, specific references to these have been included in the text, diagram and tables. Many opportunities still remain for further research in this field and future research workers, who may wish to delve more deeply into various aspects of it, will find much useful material on the 19th-century trade and shipping history of Hull in the primary sources listed below. A select bibliography of the main relevant works, published or unpublished, is also appended, but those interested should also consult: A. G. Dickens and K. A. MacMahon, *A Guide to Regional Studies on the East Riding of Yorkshire and the City of Hull* (1956); R. F. Drewery, compiler, *A Select List of Books on Hull and District* (1968); and K. J. Allison, editor, *The Victoria History of the County of York, East Riding*, vol. I (City of Kingston upon Hull) (1969).

Sources:

A. MSS.

1. *Official*

i. Hull outletter books (containing mainly correspondence between the outports and London and including much descriptive material and some statistical data)

H.M. Customs and Excise, King's Beam House, London E.C.3.

ii. Registers of Ships (from 1804) (these give details of tonnages, ownership, etc. of all registered vessels)

H.M. Customs and Excise, Custom House, Hull.

2. *Other primary sources*

i. Banking records: Bank of England

Documents, correspondence, etc. relating to the Hull branch of the Bank, 1828-75. Later material not yet available for research purposes: Bank of England, London.

Hull Banking Co.	Directors' Minute Books, 1833-94: Midland Bank Ltd., London.
Hull Savings Bank	Annual Reports, Minute Books, etc. from 1817: Hull Savings Bank.

ii. Other business records*

C. & W. Earle and Earle's Shipbuilding and Engineering Co. Ltd.	Annual Reports: M.M.; Yard List: H.C.L.; other papers: H.U.L. and P.R.O.
Russia Co.	List of freemen: Bodleian Library, Oxford.
Martin Samuelson	List of ships built: M.M.
Thomas Wilson, Sons & Co. Ltd.	List of ships' particulars: Ellerman's Wilson Line Ltd., Hull.

iii. Huffam MSS.
Collection of miscellaneous information relating to trade and shipping of Hull and the Hull docks, 1775-1907: H.U.L. microtexts 237 and 238.

iv. Whaling records
Log books: M.M. and H.C.L. (latter on microfilm); notebook of whaling statistics, 1772-1842: H.C.L.; Whale Shipowners' Association Minute Book (1813-25): M.M.

B. PRINTED

1. *Official*

Numbers and tonnages of vessels entering Hull 1808-1832: *A. & P.* 1833 XXXIII.

A return of the number of vessels entered inwards and cleared outwards at each of the twelve principal ports of the U.K. from 1816-50 *inclusive: A. & P.* 1851 LII.

Tables of Revenue, Population, Commerce, etc. of the U.K. Part III, 1820-33: *A. & P.* 1835 XLIX.

Tables of Revenue, Population, Commerce, etc. (known as Porter's Tables) 1834-52: *S.P.*

---

* Some printed material is included in these collections.

Trade and Navigation Accounts and Annual Statements of Trade,
1853-1900: 1853 in *S.P.* as part of Finance Accounts, then annually
in *S.P.*

*A statement of the declared value of the exports of each of the twelve
principal ports of the U.K. for the longest term of years for which
information is available in the period* 1816-50 (N.B. for Hull it is from
1833): *A. &. P.* 1851 LII.

Quantities and values of the ten principal articles exported in 1850 *and*
1851 *from each of the ports of London, Liverpool, Hull, Bristol,
Southampton, Newcastle, Glasgow and specifying the total declared
values of the exports. A. & P.:* 1852-3 XCIX.
*Statement of the declared value of the exports of each of the twelve
principal ports of the U.K.:*

> 1851-2   *A. & P.* 1854 LX.
> 1854   *A. & P.* 1854-5 XLVI.
> 1855   *A. & P.* 1856 LV.
> 1856   *A. & P.* Sess. 2 1857 XXXIX.

Customs Tariffs of the U.K. 1800-97 (for details of the real values of
exports of produce and manufacture of the U.K. from 1805):
A. & P. 1898 LXXXV.

Bills of Entry and Shipping Lists for 1832, 1835-53, 1858-98: H.C.L.
(These contain very detailed analyses of the articles imported to and
exported from Hull).

2. *Other primary printed sources*

Hull Chamber of Commerce:

> *Annual Reports,* 1839 onwards; *Hull General Price Current,
> Imports etc.* 1853 onwards. (These include data from 1845
> relating to Hull imports and also give useful annual summaries
> on the state of trade): Hull Chamber of Commerce and the
> Price Current also on microfilm at H.C.L.

Lloyd's Registers of Shipping
> 19th century: H.C.L.

Bibliography

L. M. BROWN, 'Modern Hull', in *V.C.H. Yorks. E.R. I*, pp. 215-86.

G. S. CLARK, 'The Location and Development of the Hull Fishing
Industry', University of Hull, M.Sc. thesis (1957).

W. G. EAST, 'The Port of Kingston upon Hull during the Industrial
Revolution', *Economica*, vol. xi (1931).

EASTERN MORNING NEWS, *The Trade and Commerce of Hull and its Ships and Shipowners, past and present* (2nd edn.) (1878).

W. GAWTRESS, *Report of an Inquiry into the Corporation of Hull* (1834) (This contains a useful statistical appendix including data on shipping (coastal and foreign) and imports etc.).

J. T. JENKINS, 'Bibliography of Whaling', *Journal of the Society for the Bibliography of Natural History*, vol. ii, part 4 (1948).

D. F. KING, 'The major provincial seaports of England 1800-1850, excluding their coastwise trade', University of Manchester, M.A. (Econ) thesis (1959).

B. LUBBOCK, *The Arctic Whalers* (1937).

H. E. C. NEWHAM, EDITOR, *Hull as a Coal Port* (1913).

F. H. PEARSON, *The Early History of Hull Steam Shipping* (1896).

Acknowledgements

I am especially indebted to my colleague Mr. D. M. Woodward for his invaluable comments and most helpful suggestions on earlier drafts of this study. I also wish to record my deep appreciation of the guidance I received from Mr. John Saville, Reader in Economic History at the University, when preparing the original thesis material. My grateful thanks are also due to Mr. J. B. Fisher, of the Department of Geography, Hull University, for photographic reproduction of the diagram and to Dr. W. H. Chaloner, of Manchester University, and Dr. W. M. Mathew, of Leicester University, for some information relating to the traffic in bones. I have received much assistance from Mrs. Jennifer Stanley, former Local History Librarian, Kingston upon Hull City Library, Mr. W. J. Hope, Secretary of the Hull Chamber of Commerce, Mr. W. W. Shepherdson, Ellerman's Wilson Line Ltd., and members of H.M. Customs and Excise Staff, Hull. For permission to use banking records I am particularly grateful to Messrs. R. A. Woods and E. M. Kelly, Bank of England, Mr. J. E. Wadsworth, Economic Consultant, Midland Bank Ltd., Dr. H. I. Loten, Pro-Chancellor, Hull University, and Mr. S. T. Kershaw, Actuary, Hull Savings Bank. I am also indebted to Miss Jillian Crowther, Local History Librarian, Kingston upon Hull City Library, who located the illustration used for the cover.